Daisy Bates

Daisy Bates. *Daisy Bates Papers (MC 582), Series 4, Subseries 1, Box 9, #6. Special Collections, University of Arkansas Libraries, Fayetteville.*

Daisy Bates

Civil Rights Crusader

Amy Polakow

LINNET BOOKS • NORTH HAVEN, CONNECTICUT

First published 2003 as a Linnet Book,
an imprint of The Shoe String Press, Inc.
2 Linsley Street, North Haven, Connecticut 06473.
www.shoestringpress.com

Library of Congress Cataloging-in-Publication Data

Polakow, Amy, 1958–
    Daisy Bates : civil rights crusader / by Amy Polakow.
      p. cm.
    Summary: A biography of the civil rights activist who led the fight to inte-
grate schools in Little Rock, Arkansas, during the 1950s.
    Includes bibliographical references and index.
    ISBN 0–208–02513–8 (alk. paper)
    1. Bates, Daisy–Juvenile literature. 2. School integration–Arkansas–Little
Rock–Juvenile literature. 3. Central High School (Little Rock, Ark.)–Juvenile
literature. 4. African American civil right workers–Arkansas–Little Rock–
Biography–Juvenile literature. 5. Civil rights workers–Arkansas–Little
Rock–Biography–Juvenile literature. 6. Little Rock (Ark.)–Race relations–
Juvenile literature. [1. Bates, Daisy. 2. Civil rights workers. 3. School integra-
tion–Arkansas–History. 4. Little Rock (Ark.)–Race relations. 5. African
American–Biography. 6. Women–Biography.] I. Title.

F419.L7 P65 2003
379.2'63'092–dc21
    [B]   2002031276

The paper in this publication meets the
minimum requirements of American National
Standard for Information Sciences–Permanence
of Paper for Printed Library Materials,
ANSI/NISO Z39.48–1992 (R1997). ∞

Designed by Dutton and Sherman

Printed in the United States of America

To Sari, Matt, Scott, and all who believe
in a higher power of reason, integrity, and justice.

Contents

Author's Note / ix

Acknowledgments / xi

1. *Opportunity Knocks* / 1

2. *Huttig* / 6

3. *Shattered Innocence* / 12

4. *Revenge* / 17

5. *Birth of the* State Press / 26

6. *Days of Change* / 35

7. *Tension Builds in Little Rock* / 43

8. *Chaos in Little Rock* / 54

9. *Ripples from Little Rock* / 66

10. *Mitchellville* / 74

11. *Freedom Sparks* / 82

*Afterword: What Happened to the
Little Rock Nine?* / 91

Notes / 95

Selected Bibliography / 99

Further Reading / 103

Index / 105

Author's Note

Readers will find in this book ideas about race and racial epithets that are not acceptable in society today. These things are part of Daisy Bates's story, however. It would be both historically wrong, and disrespectful of the struggle for African American civil rights, to try to pretend that they did not exist.

Acknowledgments

M any thanks to my editors, Diantha Thorpe and Colleen Spata for their patience, knowledge, guidance, and for taking a chance on me. I am grateful as well for the guidance of Linda Leopold Strauss, my mentor and coach.

I would like to thank Daisy's relatives; Lenda Gatson Hunter, Sharon and Cleodis Gatson, and Reginald Carpenter; Daisy's "foster" daughter Linda Mitchell; and Daisy's friend Ari Merretazon for their trust, friendship, and for sharing their loving stories and memories of Daisy with me.

I would like to thank Bob Besom, of the Shiloh Museum, Springdale, Arkansas for making a special trip to bring me valuable information and photographs from his personal collection of historical artifacts from Southern Arkansas, and for donating several photos for this book. Also, thanks to the National Association for the Advancement of Colored People (NAACP) for permission to use the photograph on page 47.

I would like to thank Andrea Cantrell, Anne Prichard, and Michael Dabrishus, of the University of Arkansas Libraries, Special Collections Division, Fayetteville, Arkansas; Harry Miller, Jim Hanson, Dee Anna Grimsrud, and the staff of the State Historical Society of Wisconsin;

and Mary Jo Taylor and the Vernon Area Public librarians; and Bobbie Norman, of Dumas, Arkansas, for their generous assistance with my research.

Finally, I would like to thank my parents, who fostered my belief that I could accomplish anything if I was willing to work hard enough for it; Jenny, for providing me with the time and space to follow my dreams; and my friends and family, who brighten my world.

Chapter 1

Opportunity Knocks

I n September 1957, in Little Rock, Arkansas, fifteen-year-old Elizabeth Eckford approached her new school for the very first time. She was African American and she was terrified. There was not another black face anywhere in sight. The white mob that blocked her access to the school when she arrived hated her. They didn't want black students in their school. Clutching her books tight to her chest, Elizabeth held her head high as she walked down the street toward Central High School.

The angry mob of hundreds of white children and adults crowded in around her, tighter and tighter the closer she got. They screamed obscenities, threw things, and spit at her. They threatened her life. "Get her! Get the nigger out of here! Hang her! Lynch her,"[1] they shouted. They were convinced that black students had no right to attend their school.

As scared as she was, Elizabeth believed that the guards lined up around the perimeter of the school were there to protect her. If she could just make it down the block and across Park Street to where they stood, surely they would keep her safe. When she started to cross the street she began to worry. Why didn't the guards step forward to protect her? Where were the other eight black students who were supposed to have joined her that morning? Elizabeth approached one of the guards who lined the empty sidewalk in front of Central High School. Staring down at her he pointed across the street, back into the mob from where she had come.

"You mean I should walk over there and down the street?"[2] she asked him. The soldier nodded yes. With trembling but determined steps, Elizabeth left the protected sidewalk in front of the school, and started back across the street. As she walked the crowd pressed in on her, forcing her into the middle of the street. By the time she reached the school, the crowd had bullied her back onto the sidewalk with the soldiers. Elizabeth tried to pass between the soldiers several times, but each time they moved together and prevented her from passing. Finally, she tried to walk past a guard who had just let a few white girls down the front sidewalk leading to the school entrance. The guard planted his weapon in front of her and refused to let her pass. Elizabeth turned her panicked face to the angry crowd. She spotted an elderly white woman who she thought for an instant would help her, but as Elizabeth looked at her with pleading eyes, the woman spat at her.

Two blocks away, a woman who had come to love Elizabeth like a daughter waited with the other black children who were supposed to attend Central High School that day. The woman, Daisy Bates, felt sick over the reports on the radio about a single black child being attacked by the angry whites. Daisy felt responsible for protecting Elizabeth. It had been mostly due to her efforts that Elizabeth had come to this school in the first place.

Daisy Bates had worked tirelessly and with great passion for years so that the black children in her town would be given the same educational opportunities as the white children. She had risked everything–her job, her friends and family, even her life–for this day. She had given up countless nights of sleep. She had received hundreds of letters and telephone calls begging her not to mix the races, and threatening her if she tried. One night someone threw a rock through Daisy's window that landed just inches from her head. It had a message attached that threatened to blow her house up. A few nights after this, someone in a passing car fired a round of gunshots across the front of her house. Some of the shots bounced off the brick front of the house, but one smashed through the picture window and lodged in the living room wall. And only days before both of these incidents, some of those opposed to integration had burned a cross on Daisy Bates's lawn.

Daisy understood that there were a lot of people in Little Rock who would like to see her dead for her efforts to integrate their schools. For nearly one hundred years since the Civil War had rendered slavery illegal, segregation had been a way for southern whites to maintain their perceived superiority and their real social and economic advantages over black people. What Daisy could not understand was how people could want to harm innocent children like Elizabeth. How could hundreds of full-grown adults act like this? Elizabeth was just an isolated, defenseless girl, going to school, as was her lawful right.

Daisy Bates had done everything she could think of to ensure the safety of the nine African American students she had prepared to go to Central High School in that fall of 1957. She had attended dozens of meetings and court proceedings for the past three years so she would know exactly what to expect. She had spent the entire summer working with the students who would come to be known as the "Little Rock Nine." She had coached them about what might happen, and how to deal with people who provoked them. If white students teased them, kicked them, or threatened them in any way, they were not allowed to retaliate. They were to walk on as if they didn't even notice, and hold their heads high, just as Elizabeth was doing now. Later, they could report any offenses to the proper authorities, who were bound by law to deal with them as necessary.

Daisy Bates had prepared the Little Rock Nine in many other ways as well. She had helped them select and plan for their classes. She had taught them how to speak and act toward reporters. She had even helped them choose what to wear that day after finding ways for the students to afford new clothes so they would look their very best.

While Daisy anticipated and planned for resistance from the community, it is unlikely that she was prepared for the magnitude of conflict that unfolded in the last few days before school was to start. Consumed with concern for the very lives of the students in her care, Daisy stayed up nearly all night long before school was to start, coordinating everything–from where they would meet and who would walk with them to which door they would enter and what order they would walk in. She demanded that local policemen protect them and she pleaded with local ministers to escort the children the rest of the way to the school, where the policemen were not allowed. Fearing a mob scene like the one Elizabeth was enduring right now, Daisy Bates had tried to call each of the nine children in the middle of the night to ask them all to gather in one place and walk together to school the next morning. But Elizabeth Eckford's family didn't have a phone. Daisy had planned to go to Elizabeth's house very early in the morning to tell her where to meet the rest of the students, but after a night of no sleep, Daisy was waylaid by reporters, and distracted by phone calls, news reports, and other commotions. Now she waited two blocks away in helpless fear as she observed the catastrophic results of the one detail that had slipped through her fingers.

As it turned out, Elizabeth Eckford escaped harm that morning. But she didn't get through the doors of Central High School that day, nor did any of the other African American children who were supposed to be there. They would make it there eventually, but it would take more of Daisy's help and the protection of the 101st Airborne Infantry of the United States Army.

The story of the Little Rock Nine was so explosive and heroic that it became front-page news across the United States for that entire year. Even today those nine students are famous for their determination and courage. But at the end of the 1957-58 school year, most people in Little Rock would have told you that the biggest reason Central High was integrated in 1957 was because Daisy Bates willed it. The determination of one woman, nine students, their families, and a few other people had prevailed over long years of forced separation of black people from white and over the desire of millions of people who wanted it to stay that way.

When Daisy Bates was a child, she never understood or accepted the reasons people gave when she asked why white people were treated so much better than black people. Once, her father said, "This is the way things are today, but someway, somehow, somebody is going to make it different."[3] He was right—things are different today and Daisy Bates is one of the reasons why.

Chapter 2

Huttig

lthough many books and magazine articles about Daisy
Bates report that she was born in 1920, or even in 1922, her
birth certificate states that she was born on November 11,
1914. This confusion is probably due to a combination of things. Birth
records, particularly those of African Americans, were very poorly
maintained in the South of the early 1900s. In addition, there was
much secrecy, and feelings of great shame regarding the identity of
Daisy's birth parents. The fact that her parents were not married
when she was born was further complicated when her mother, Millie
Riley, was murdered by white men. Her father, Hezekiah C. Gatson,
had then fled in a state of helpless rage at the injustice and shame he
felt. He was powerless to avenge Millie's death without risking his life
and his little daughter's life as well. Orlee and Susie Smith, very close
friends of Daisy's parents, took Daisy in and raised her as their own
daughter when Hezekiah fled. Daisy grew up thinking that the
Smiths were her parents.

Daisy was born in Huttig, a very small town in southern
Arkansas. Huttig was called a "sawmill town" because life there cen-
tered around the Union Saw Mill Company, where almost everyone
in town worked.

Daisy's adoptive father, Orlee Smith, was a strong but gentle man. He adored Daisy, and they spent a lot of time together—talking, hiking in the woods, and fishing. Orlee Smith worked as a lumber grader at the Union Saw Mill. Most of the jobs available to African Americans at the mill were physical labor, like cutting trees and transporting logs. A lumber grader inspected the boards that were cut, and graded them according to size, quality, and kind of wood. Lumber graders were required to know a lot about trees and the lumber business. This was the most difficult and highest paying job an African American could hold at the sawmill. Mr. Smith wasn't paid with money, though. He was paid in coupons that could only be used at the sawmill store, called the Commissary, where everyone in town bought just about everything they needed.

Daisy's adoptive mother, Susie Smith, was tall and kind, but she was a strict disciplinarian with Daisy, who was frequently spanked, switched with a stick, or made to stand facing the corner for her outspoken and tomboy-like ways. On the other hand, as an only child, Daisy was indulged by both her parents. She didn't have to share their attention or any of her things with brothers and sisters, and she was used to getting what she wanted.

Daisy and her father talked about a lot of things together, but one thing they never discussed when she was a young child was the difficult and painful subject of race relations in their town. There were very definite, and often unspoken, rules that everybody followed concerning relationships between black- and white-skinned people.

"As I grew up in Huttig, I learned that the difference between the races was symbolized by the color of the buildings," Daisy once said as an adult. "Everything in the Negro community was painted a dull, drab red and everything in the white community was white."[1] Blacks and whites lived close to each other and worked together, but they were separated in many ways. The grocery store and the post office on Main Street divided "White town" from what was called "Nigra town," where African Americans lived.

Most of the white homes had indoor toilets, a far cry from the outhouse in Daisy's backyard. The whites' homes also tended to be roomier, and some even had stairs leading to a second floor. Daisy's home was a small "shotgun" house. From the front door, a person could look straight through the house and out the window of the back door. These houses were often just one large room, though Daisy's home had a separate bedroom and a small enclosure for a bathtub.

There were other separations as well. Black people were allowed only in the last two rows of the movie theater. There were separate churches for the separate races. Well-maintained, the white church was decorated with the finest furniture. In addition to religious services, white folks attended public performances at the church or in a special community center provided for them by the owners of the sawmill. In contrast, the black churches were old drafty buildings. Their "community center" was the stuffy, barren second floor of the white community center. African Americans were not allowed in the public library or in most restaurants and stores. They were required to sit in the last few rows of city buses and to drink from a separate water fountain.

Daisy attended a different school than the white children who lived near her. The school white children went to was a brand new white brick building with a large play yard outside. It was modeled after a beautiful new school in a neighboring state. In contrast, Daisy's school was a tiny, run-down, two-room building, with no bathrooms, no play yard, and a potbellied stove to keep the students warm. Though her teacher would stop the lesson frequently to load more wood into the stove, most of the kids still wore their coats all day. The books they used were old ripped ones that the white school didn't want anymore.

Daisy was always an inquisitive child. She observed everything, and was filled with unanswered questions about why these great differences existed between black and white people. Why did black and white children play together and walk to and from school together, but black children could only go to inferior schools? Why were white adults addressed with titles of respect, such as "Mrs." and "Mr.," while black adults were addressed by their first names, or even, simply, "Boy" or "Girl?" Why did she have lots of white friends, but her parents had none? In fact, there didn't seem to be any friendships between black and white adults, only between children. When did these friendships stop, and why?

Despite the injustices that Daisy observed, she was a proud and happy child. She had lots of friends, both black and white, and lots of things to keep her busy. She and her friends spent a lot of time at the Commissary, the general store owned by the Union Saw Mill Company. This was the largest general store in the whole state of Arkansas. It had food, candy, clothes, and toys. It was the commercial and social center of Huttig. Daisy and her friends would pool their pennies to buy winding balls, peppermint sticks, and other trinkets. Her family bought all their holiday gifts there each year.

Daisy especially loved flowers and gardening. Each spring, she collected beautiful bouquets of bright yellow cowslips and orangey-red Indian paintbrushes that bloomed in the open fields. In her own garden at home, she planted roses and zinnias. Everyone in the neighborhood knew that the beautiful garden was tended by young Daisy, and not by her mother, as was usually the case. This made her particularly proud.

Daisy loved animals as well, and had an assortment of cats and dogs while she was growing up. She also loved to fish, and ride the old gray horse at her grandmother's farm. She was a tomboy and could climb the mulberry tree in her backyard as high as any of the boys in her neighborhood. She loved games, and she particularly liked to win what she played. After a few lessons with the neighborhood marble champ, Daisy beat him at his own game.

Susie Smith was a very religious woman, and Daisy inherited a deep appreciation for religion from her as she matured. But as a child, Daisy's impish sense of fun far outweighed her respect for religion. Once, when Daisy was ill, her mother brought the Church Sister Meeting to Daisy's bedside to pray for her. One of Daisy's friends had brought her some guinea pigs earlier that afternoon to make her feel better. Daisy hid the guinea pigs under her covers because she knew her mother would not approve. As the church women gathered around her bed in prayer, Daisy was struck with an undeniable urge: She slyly released the guinea pigs onto the floor, where they soon transformed the prayer session into frenzied, foot-stomping chaos. Daisy was so delighted with the performance that she thought it was worth the spanking she paid for it. "The ladies," Daisy later claimed, "although convinced that I certainly needed prayer, decided to do their praying for me elsewhere."[2]

One day, when Daisy was seven years old, Susie asked her to go to the butcher and get some pork chops for dinner. Daisy was pleased. What a chance to show her mom how grown-up she was! She skipped all the way to the market. There were several white adults in the store when she arrived. She waited until they had all been served before politely telling the butcher what she wanted. The butcher started to reach for the chops when a few more white adults came in. He stopped what he was doing and took care of them instead. This bothered Daisy. She was anxious to get home and help her mother make dinner. Since they were adults, though, Daisy knew she had to wait. While the butcher was filling their orders, a white child who Daisy knew entered the store.

"What do you want, little girl?" the butcher asked when the adults had left.

Daisy smiled and said, "I told you before, a pound of center-cut pork chops."[3]

"I'm not talking to you!"[4] snapped the butcher, and he proceeded to serve the little white girl. When everyone else had left the store, the butcher cut a few slices of the worst meat he had, angrily shoved the package at Daisy, and said, "Niggers have to wait 'til I wait on the white people. Now take your meat and get out of here!"[5]

Daisy cried all the way home. She felt afraid, angry, and ashamed of what had happened at the butcher shop. When she got home, she tearfully told her parents and begged them to take the fatty meat back to the butcher. Daisy didn't understand their reaction. They seemed as upset as she was, but they sat her down and told her that there was nothing they could do. If they went to the market to complain, there would be trouble for the whole family. Daisy didn't understand what they meant. But what she did understand was that the reason she wasn't shown the same respect and courtesy by the butcher that he showed to the whites was only because of the color of her skin.

Daisy never discussed the incident with her parents again, but that night she prayed that the butcher would die. She no longer trusted any white people—even her friends.

Chapter 3

Shattered Innocence

Daisy's carefree, happy childhood ended quite suddenly, when she was eight years old. She was sitting on the porch steps of a neighborhood friend, and one of the older boys she didn't like very much started pulling on her braids. Daisy got upset and said she was going home. The boy said, "You always act so uppity. If you knew what happened to your mother, you wouldn't act so stuck up." The boy then told her that the woman she lived with wasn't her real mother. Daisy's real mom, he said, was killed by white men.

"That's a story and you're a mean and nasty old boy," Daisy shot back, and then she started to cry. She was stunned.

Hearing the commotion, the mother of the house she was at came out and said, "Don't believe nothing that no-good boy says."[1] But it was too late. That night Daisy realized that she didn't look very much like either one of her parents. She started to remember lots of other things too, like when her mother was talking to a salesman one day. The salesman had asked her mom if she had heard from Daisy's dad. Her mother had said no, and then she told the man that they hadn't told Daisy yet. Daisy didn't think much about it back then, but suddenly it made sense. The salesman must have been talking about her *real* dad.

Daisy didn't tell her parents what she had learned right away, but she was terribly upset. She stopped playing with her friends and spent all her time alone. Her parents thought she was ill, and started giving her medicine to make her feel better. Of course it didn't help. Finally, she confided what she knew to her cousin one day when he came to visit. He was angry that Daisy had been so carelessly informed of this secret that the whole town had struggled to keep, but he didn't deny the story. Instead, he told Daisy how it happened.

One night when Daisy was a baby, a white man came to her house to talk to her mom. The man told her that Daisy's dad had been badly hurt while working at the sawmill, and needed help. After asking a neighbor to watch Daisy, her mother ran out with the man.

The next morning, Daisy's dad came home from work and found her alone in the house. He had not been hurt at all, but had worked all night as he was supposed to. The neighbor told him what had happened, but by now it was clear that the man who had come to see Daisy's mother had not been telling the truth. He had made up the story just to get her mom to leave the house with him. Everyone in the neighborhood searched for Daisy's mother. They found her body lying in a nearby pond.

White people in Huttig talked freely among themselves about the tragedy, either unaware or unconcerned that their African American hired help listened to everything they said. Almost everyone in Daisy's community heard the same story that was being told up in "white town." Three white men had lured her mother away from home and raped her, then they killed her and ran away.

Crimes like this against black people were not unusual in the early part of the century. The sheriff never did much of an investigation and the matter was quickly dropped. This was a common response to such crimes for many years to come.

Daisy's father knew that nothing would be done about Millie's murder and that if he pressed the issue, his life would be in danger as well. He was so tormented, angry, and ashamed that he left town and never came back.

The truth about her birth mother made Daisy so sad that none of the things she loved to do held her interest anymore. She didn't fish or play games or dolls with her friends. And her beautiful garden came to symbolize death. One day when the last brilliant red rose flowered open on its stem, she sobbed to Susie, "All the other flowers were dead and my rose will die, too."[2] Her mother was very worried about her, but Mr. Smith reassured his wife that Daisy just needed some time.

Initially, Orlee and Susie Smith didn't discuss the story of Daisy's birth mother with her. In those days, it was very unusual for parents to talk about painful issues like death with children. One day, Daisy and her father were walking in the woods together. This was an activity that usually made her feel peaceful and lighthearted, but after hearing about her birth mom, she never felt happy anymore. No one had mentioned Millie since the day Daisy had learned the truth and she had lots of questions burning inside her.

"Daddy, who killed my mother?" Daisy asked. "Why did they kill her?"[3]

Orlee took awhile to think. The answer he gave Daisy about her mother was not entirely accurate, and Daisy would not learn the full truth until many years later, but Orlee did the best he could to explain how many years of blacks being treated as inferiors by whites had led to her mother's murder. In a sad, soft voice he explained to her that her mother had been particularly at risk for sexual abuse because she was beautiful and she was proud. She held her head high all the time and didn't look meekly at the ground when talking to white men. Her mother would not have let these men attack her without a fight. This might have further provoked them to kill her. Orlee then explained many more things to Daisy, about how black people were abused and humiliated in the South, but Daisy didn't hear him. Her mind was stuck on the men who had killed her mother. From that day on, she was determined to find them.

Now the wedge that had come between Daisy and her white friends after her experience with the butcher grew. Even her African American friends held little interest for her. One day, Daisy was in the Commissary with a black friend. A white friend whom she had known for many years tapped her on the back and offered to share her pennies with Daisy. All the anger and confusion over her mother's death erupted and Daisy slapped her friend in the face before she even knew what she was doing. "Don't you ever touch me again! I don't want your penny!"[4] Daisy snarled at the girl. Immediately afterward, Daisy was stricken with panic. In addition to feeling confused and sorry about how she had treated her friend, she was terrified that she or her family would be punished because she had struck a white person. What if her girlfriend told someone? Would they come after Daisy and her family? Would they hurt her?

After that, Daisy was afraid to even speak to her white girlfriend again. She was so scared that she never even told her mother about what happened. Daisy's fear was reinforced by what she had heard about another family in her town. As the story was told to Daisy, a white girl came up behind a black boy on the sidewalk and said, "Get off the walk, nigger, and let me pass." The black boy responded, "You don't own all the sidewalk. There's plenty [of] room for you to pass, and if you think I'm going to get off the sidewalk into the muddy street, you're crazy."[5] The girl's father went to the boy's house that evening with a leather strap and forced the boy's father to beat his son so he would learn to respect white people. The black family moved away after that.

As an adult, Daisy compared notes with some of her friends about similar experiences they had as children. A white friend told Daisy that when she was a little girl growing up in the South, she had invited her best friend, a black boy, for a tea party. As most young children do from time to time with their friends, she decided to play a joke on him. Instead of frosting the cookies with regular frosting, she made a foul-tasting paste of flour, water, and salt. She couldn't wait to see the awful face he would make as he spit out the cookie and realized it was a joke. To her amazement, the boy ate the cookie without any expression at all! The little girl was horrified and embarrassed. As Daisy grew, she learned to understand that many African Americans were very careful in their relationships with white people because there was a long history of encountering serious trouble if they became upset or angry in any way with a white person. These inequalities and tensions quietly churned under the surface of interactions between black and white people in Huttig and in many places in America.

Chapter 4

Revenge

One day when Daisy was nine years old, she was at the Commissary and she felt a man staring at her. When she stared back at the man, he looked puzzled at first, then frightened. Daisy became increasingly preoccupied with this man over the next few months. The man was white, and Daisy usually found him sitting outside the Commissary on a wooden bench. He was always drunk, and he became more and more disheveled as the months progressed. He appeared to be equally struck by Daisy, and would look at her as if he knew her but could hardly believe what he was seeing. Daisy had been told many times that she looked exactly like her mother, and she began to suspect that this man had something to do with her mother's murder. Her suspicion only increased as the man's fear of her became more apparent. She liked to stare him down because she could see how uncomfortable it made him. Once he shouted at her to stop staring at him and he jumped up from the bench to come after her. Then he sank down in his seat again and begged, "Go away! Haven't I suffered enough?"[1]

One day around Christmas in 1923, a few months after the beginning of her silent war with the white man whom she secretly called "Drunken Pig," Daisy was in the Commissary looking at Christmas toys. Two men from the town came in and noticed the drunk man slouched on the bench. They both appeared to know him. One of them commented on how terrible the drunk man looked, and asked his companion what had happened to him. The second man replied, "I got an idea what's happened. You heard about that colored woman they found in the mill-pond a few years ago? I heard he was involved…leastwise, he started to drink about then, and he's been getting worse and worse ever since. He's about hit rock bottom…."[2]

This conversation confirmed Daisy's suspicion about why Drunken Pig was so interested in her. She hated white people even more after that, and she blamed him for everything—for killing her mother, for wrecking her happiness, and for making her hate white people. She began to spend all her free time at the store, trying to make Drunken Pig miserable with her silent, accusing stares. It seemed to work because he looked worse and worse.

Very soon, Daisy didn't want to do anything else except be in that store. Her parents knew that anger was eating away at her, but they didn't know about the man in the Commissary. Orlee and Susie Smith assumed that Daisy's distress was due to her mother's murder, not from suspecting she knew the person who had done it. They understood what a big shock the news had been, and they were patiently waiting for Daisy to feel better.

One day when Daisy came to the Commissary, Drunken Pig was nowhere to be found. His bench was empty. An old white man who often occupied a chair on the porch of the Commissary had befriended Daisy and the other children who frequented the store. He had watched her silent battle with Drunken Pig, and he told Daisy that the man wouldn't be back again; he had died. Daisy was very upset, perhaps because he had been her only link to her birth mother and she had built her whole world around hating him. Now he was gone. The old white man put his arm around Daisy's shoulder as she sobbed and he gave her some candy. Then, as most adults would

Many whites in the South didn't want integration. Mobs of students and their parents shouted in defiance and threatened Elizabeth Eckford as she attempted to enter all-white Central High School in Little Rock. *Photo by Francis Miller. Courtesy of TimePix.*

Daisy grew up in the small town of Huttig in a "shotgun" house. These houses got their name from the observation that you could shoot a gun through the front door and the bullet would come right out the back door a split-second later. Below: the commissary of the Union Saw Mill Company dominated the town; it is the large building in the center. This is where eight-year-old Daisy confronted "Drunken Pig." *Courtesy of Bob Besom of the Shiloh Museum of Ozark History.*

Daisy as a young woman, in her early years with L.C. *Daisy Bates Papers (MC 582), Series 4, Subseries 1, Box 9, #1. Special Collections, University of Arkansas Libraries, Fayetteville.*

L.C. Bates was the inspiration in Daisy's life, along with Martin Luther King, Jr., and Mahatma Gandhi. *Courtesy of the Wisconsin Historical Society, Daisy Bates Collection, Image # Whi-5001.*

In the segregated South, "separate" was not "equal" in any way, as these drinking fountains make clear. *Photo by Elliott Erwitt. Courtesy of Magnum Photos.*

have done in those days, he told her to forget about it, and sent her home.

Daisy was so despondent over the death of Drunken Pig that she cried all night and wished she could die, too. The months passed and she was still miserable. Her parents felt increasingly unable to help her. Finally, Orlee went to the Commissary where the old man explained what had happened. After hearing the story, Orlee thought perhaps his daughter needed to get away from Huttig and all the bad memories during her summer vacations from school. He sent her to stay with her grandmother on a farm in eastern Arkansas. Sometimes she went to stay with friends or relatives, and once in awhile she traveled with her parents to other states. At one point Orlee sent her to Canada, where he had friends, for a short time. He knew that African

Americans were freer and more respected in the North. He hoped the visit would help heal his daughter's heart. It did. Daisy learned that many white people were decent, but the hurt was still so deep that she couldn't really trust white people in general.

She was in her teens when Daisy met a man who also helped heal her heart. Lucius Christopher Bates, L.C. as he was known, first came to Daisy's house to sell insurance to her father. L.C. was a young man, thirteen years older than Daisy. He fast became a family friend and would often visit, bringing small trinkets to Daisy, her mom, and her dad. He took them to the movies, and he had his own car, which impressed Daisy. She was drawn to him from the beginning, but L.C. was much older, and when they first met, his thoughts were on other things. "She was nothing but a kid then,"[3] L.C. said later in an interview.

What L.C. was thinking about was his dream of being a newspaper reporter. He had attended Wilberforce University in Ohio, one of the few colleges that accepted African Americans, and had studied journalism. Upon graduation, he had worked as a reporter in Colorado and several other states, but finding and keeping a job as a reporter was a constant struggle. Those days were early on in the Great Depression, a time when getting and keeping a job was difficult for everybody, but most of all for black people who wanted a profession. L.C. eventually turned to selling insurance, traveling all over the Midwest to make a living.

One summer when Daisy was a teenager and away visiting friends, her mother sent for her because Orlee was very ill. He was dying of cancer, but before he died he said something to Daisy that changed her life forever. The very last time they were together in the hospital, her father told her he knew she was still filled with hatred. He told her it was wrong to hate all white people just because they were white. It was okay to hate the horrible things that some white people had done to Negroes throughout history, but she had to use her hate to change things, or she would be uselessly wasting her time and energy. He told Daisy not to expect that changing race relations in the United States would be an easy thing to do. It would take a long time, and the first African Americans to speak out would be very much alone. But he believed that one day other blacks would join the fight, and together, they would make a difference. They would change the world to one where all people, regardless of their race, were truly free and equal.

Orlee Smith didn't have a lot of possessions to pass on to his daughter when he died. But Daisy knew he was passing on the most important thing in the world–his desire to make the world a better place for African Americans. She believed that she had the will and the strength to make her father's vision come true.

As a child, Daisy had felt very much alone with her anger about the way blacks were treated by the white world. Much of the black community probably felt the same way, but few talked about it or showed it the way Daisy did. Shortly after Orlee died, she became romantically involved with L.C. Bates and learned that he shared her feelings about racism, but for different reasons.

L.C. had been the only African American in the otherwise all-white school he had attended in the North as a boy. He grew up without the poverty or prejudice that most southern blacks experienced, and he knew what it felt like to be treated with respect. When, as a young adult, he suddenly encountered the more prevalent racist attitudes that Daisy had lived with all along in the South, he decided to devote his life to righting these wrongs. He believed that much of the trouble between blacks and whites was due to a lack of communication. L.C. thought that this lack of understanding between the races was the crux of the problem, and he believed he could help change it.

Black people knew quite a bit about the white people they worked for because they often worked in their homes, as cooks and maids, nannies and gardeners. But white people carried on in their separate world. They generally knew very little about their black employees or their concerns. In fact, much later in 1947 when Jackie Robinson became the first black baseball player ever to play in the major leagues, he was the first African American that many whites had ever seen in a respected, public role. L.C. was convinced that, as a news reporter, he could help bridge this kind of gap.

Daisy and L.C. were married in 1941, and they moved to Little Rock, Arkansas to start a new life together. L.C. was a great influence on Daisy. His wisdom, patience, and maturity were a good balance to her impulsive energy. They felt that together they would find a way to make the world a better place for African Americans.

Chapter 5

Birth of the State Press

I n the 1940s, by the time Daisy was a young woman, relations between black people and white people were considered to be pretty good in Little Rock, but much of that feeling was on the surface. Most white people didn't even entertain the idea of equal rights for blacks, and African Americans were still often treated as second-class citizens. But black people were increasingly unwilling to accept an inferior position. They didn't believe they were inferior, merely that they were being denied the opportunities to achieve the same educational and economic status that white people felt singularly entitled to.

"When I moved to Little Rock, there were 'good' relations between blacks and whites," Daisy later said. "But that meant that you stay in your place, that you know what the limits are for Daisy Bates. You couldn't stand up for your rights, because the police wouldn't protect you. I remember an incident during one of my [later] trials. I went into the restroom in the courthouse, and there was a big sign by the door that said, 'White Women Only!' I was mad, but I wasn't going to go to the basement and use the colored restroom. There was a lady in there who looked at me hard and then she said, 'Girl! You're in the wrong place!' I was so angry, I could have pushed her head down in that toilet. But I just combed my hair and powdered my face, and then I turned around and smiled and walked out."[1]

Many black people were particularly humiliated by the laws governing public bus transportation in the South. Relatively few owned cars, so the buses carried mostly African Americans. Yet the first rows of seats on every bus were reserved for white people. In many cities in the South, black people were expected to get on the bus at the front to pay their fare, then get off the bus—even if it was raining—and reenter at the back door to sit down in the back of the bus. Sometimes black people would pay their fares and get off, and the bus would leave before they could get back on. If all the seats on the bus were occupied when white people got on, the black people who were already seated were expected to give up their seats and stand.

Bus discrimination was just one of the injustices that burned Daisy up. She wanted to change all of the forms of discrimination against black people. L.C. shared these feelings and wasn't afraid to voice them. He had many connections to other people who were trying to change the discriminatory world they lived in. With L.C., Daisy now had the confidence to fight for her rights in a dignified and peaceful way. It was a goal that would consume most of her life. In a speech Daisy made many years after this time, she explained her motivation to work so hard for civil rights:

> Whenever the Negroes cry out against the denial of a decent education for their children, decent jobs, housing, equal protection under the law, the "powers that be" will pat them on the head and say, "have patience." We have been a patient people, tolerant to the point of gullibility; we are long suffering, we have endured with patience an unbelievable amount of injustice and mistreatment....The time has come for unity of purpose and for unity of action.[2]

Some of the things Daisy did to change discrimination may seem unimportant at first glance. For example, Daisy frequently and firmly insisted on being called "Mrs. Bates." One of the ways white people reminded blacks that they were considered inferior was by calling them by their first names, as one would do with a child. Sometimes white people wouldn't even bother with a black person's first name; they would just bark out, "Hey you, girl…" or "Come here, boy." Daisy refused to tolerate this.

When Daisy was a young woman, it was considered polite to refer to African Americans as Negroes. But many white people in the South flaunted their lack of respect by purposefully saying "Nigra" instead. Daisy wouldn't put up with this, either. When she heard someone say "Nigra," she stopped what she was doing and firmly said, "The word is pronounced NEE-gro, not Nigra!"[3] Even though this type of pride had gotten many black people killed, Daisy was persistent and unafraid.

She was not alone in her defiance. Many black people were tired of believing that things would get better. It had been many decades since slavery had been abolished, and yet African Americans were still largely expected to act subservient to white Americans. Organizations sprang up, and the United States government passed laws—all to enforce the rights of African Americans. But social habits and attitudes weren't easily changed by these laws. The southern states in particular tried to fight these national civil rights mandates and organizations with their own laws. In effect, these laws said that segregation was a choice that individual states were entitled to make, and they weren't going to allow the federal government or anyone else to interfere with that choice.

The National Association for the Advancement of Colored People (NAACP) was the most powerful of the civil rights organizations that existed in the 1940s. Sixty black and white people had started this organization in New York, in 1909. Their goal was "to achieve, through peaceful and lawful means, equal citizenship rights for all American citizens by eliminating segregation and discrimination in housing, employment, voting, schools, the courts, transportation, and recreation."[4]

In its earliest years, the NAACP encouraged southern black Americans to move to the northern states, where conditions were generally better; always it campaigned tirelessly to publicize and create laws preventing violence against blacks–particularly murder by lynching. In the 1890s, lynchings by racist groups such as the Ku Klux Klan claimed a new black victim every forty-eight hours. Although the NAACP did much to stop this, from 1882 to 1968 more than five thousand people–mostly black men–were lynched. In 1941, when Daisy and L.C. joined the NAACP, the United States had just entered World War II, and the NAACP was helping black military personnel obtain equal rights in the war effort. This was a volatile issue.

Thousands of black Americans went to fight in this war. They were fighting for their country, yet their country hardly recognized them as free citizens. In the South they were often not allowed to vote. For the most part, they were denied jobs that would pay enough to support a family. Their children were not allowed to attend schools that had the best teachers, programs, and facilities. They received inferior medical care, were not allowed in most restaurants or stores that served white Americans, and were often excluded from white cultural activities. Still, thousands of African Americans risked their lives fighting side by side with their white fellow Americans, so the world would be a safe place for democracy–where all people are supposed to be equal under the law and free to live the life they choose.

In some ways, World War II was a turning point in race relations in the United States. Many black Americans made a heartening discovery while fighting in this war: They found that the white British and French soldiers who were fighting alongside them didn't see them as most Americans did. These foreign soldiers showed great appreciation for their black comrades and treated them as equals. And by the time the American black soldiers came home in 1945 from risking their lives in this brutal war for world freedom, they and their families felt that they had earned their own freedom as well. Many people who had been resigned to discrimination in the United States found a new will to fight for their *own* rights. Suddenly, membership in the NAACP swelled to great numbers.

Daisy was a member in the NAACP during World War II but she was involved in many other activities—most of them civil rights efforts—as well. Primarily what consumed the majority of Daisy's time throughout the 1940s was helping L.C. establish the newspaper of his dreams.

L.C. had not given up his dream to own and run a newspaper that spoke to and about black Americans. He wanted to inform people publicly about all the acts of discrimination and police brutality that were occurring in the South. He wanted to help the white community understand the immense hardship and injustice they were inflicting on the Negro community. He believed that much of the friction between the races could be resolved with better communication, and he desperately wanted to provide the medium for that interaction.

Daisy told him she thought it was a crazy idea to discuss racism in a public paper. For the most part, individuals never dared to openly talk about the rights of Negroes. It was dangerous. Still, Daisy shared L.C.'s passion for civil rights. She was determined to be one of the fearless few who would speak out and rally her race to demand the justice they deserved. She agreed to help L.C. and they named their paper the *Arkansas State Press*, though it was widely referred to, simply, as the *State Press*.

L.C.'s past experience as a reporter helped them to get started, but they knew the success of the paper would depend mostly on how many businesses they could get to advertise in it. Money made from business ads in newspapers was often used to pay the people who worked there. For several reasons, it was going to be very tricky for Daisy and L.C. to attract and keep these advertisers.

There were very few newspapers written by and about blacks in America at that time, and none were in Little Rock, Arkansas. Many white people didn't want to hear disturbing stories about discrimination. They were afraid, angry that black people had started demanding their rights. Most of the businesses in Little Rock were owned by white people, who refused to support the aims of the *State Press*. Those that did run ads put intense pressure on Daisy and L.C. to tone down their stories about discrimination. But Daisy and L.C. refused to appease their advertisers this way. They believed that these issues needed to be aired openly and honestly. They were willing to take what they knew was the very risky gamble that they could find enough readers and advertisers who agreed with them to keep their paper alive.

Another obstacle the Bateses had to overcome was that they were trying to start a newspaper during a time when everyone had trouble making a living. People were losing their jobs left and right. Many long-standing, solid businesses went bankrupt in the Great Depression, and those that survived weren't going to take unnecessary chances. Many of them wouldn't consider spending money to advertise in a brand new paper that was run by Negroes and was upsetting many of the white people in the community.

Despite all these obstacles, the *State Press* started out with a bang. The first issue was published on May 9, 1941. In its first few months of operation the paper attracted 10,000 subscribers! To Daisy and L.C.'s surprise and great satisfaction, both black and white people were buying and reading the paper, and it was making money. Daisy spent her days poring over the hundreds of news bulletins that crossed her desk about the senseless crimes committed against Negroes. She and L.C. focused their news stories on their crusade to expose the injustice of segregation, and on rampant police brutality.

Friction between the police and the black soldiers who were stationed at the Little Rock army base during World War II was particularly intense. A year after Daisy and L.C. first started their newspaper, on March 2, 1942, there was a scuffle between the police and some black soldiers who were at the local army base for a weekend leave. The policemen were hassling the soldiers and the soldiers were demanding to know why they were being harassed. Things heated up and a policeman shot a black army officer five times, killing him. The Negro community was enraged, and would not be quiet or patient about it. Daisy wrote the following bitter and accusatory story in the *State Press*, and the white community retaliated.

City Patrolman Shoots Negro Soldier
Body Riddled While Lying on Ground

One of the most bestial murders in the annals of Little Rock occurred Sunday afternoon at 5:45 o'clock at Ninth and Gaines Streets, in front of hundreds of onlookers, when Patrolman A. J. Hay shot and mortally wounded Sergeant Thomas P. Foster, member of Company D, 92nd Engineers, stationed at Camp Robinson....When Sgt. Foster asked the Military Police why they had Pvt. Albert Glover in custody, City Policeman Hay interfered and struck Sgt. Foster with his night stick. A scuffle ensued, whereupon Policeman Hay threw Sgt. Foster to the ground and then fired five shots from his pistol into his prostrate body. Sgt. Foster died in the University Hospital five hours later....[5]

Five days after the story appeared, all the businesses in the downtown area of Little Rock canceled their advertisements with the paper, and many white subscribers canceled their subscriptions.

After that, L.C. and Daisy worked every day, all day and far into every night, to save their paper. At first, their efforts paid off. The *State Press* had lost many of its first, local advertisers, but it had also attracted huge numbers of black readers and advertisers, and new white readers from far away who were interested in the stories about civil rights. By 1945, the *State Press* had 20,000 readers and Little

Rock was beginning to acquire a reputation as liberal, or intolerant of racism. The *State Press* had helped to create this reputation.

In all her stories, Daisy didn't mince words. Four years later, she covered a story about workers who were striking at a cotton oil mill near the newspaper's office. They thought that their working conditions were unfair. They agreed not to work until the bosses responded to their complaints. They picketed, marching in front of the building with signs protesting the management. They hoped that everyone, including other workers, would support their cause by not crossing the picket line and going to work until the strike was resolved.

During this strike, one of the black picketers was killed by a white worker who had been hired to replace him. The killer was set free, with no punishment, while the black picketers were sent to jail for a year. Daisy was furious! She wrote the following story, which appeared in the *State Press* on March 29, 1946:

FTA Strikers Sentenced to Pen by a Hand-Picked Jury

Three strikers, who by all observation were guilty of no greater crime than walking on a picket line, were sentenced to one year in the penitentiary yesterday by a "hand-picked" jury, while a scab who killed a striker is free.

The prosecution was hard pressed to make a case until Judge Lawrence C. Auten instructed the jury that the pickets could be found guilty if they aided or assisted, or just stood idly by while violence occurred.

Motions to quash the indictments were overruled by the judge. These motions included protests to the fact that there were no Negroes on the jury in accordance with the law.

Appeal bond was fixed at $2,500 each. The usual bond in such cases is $1,000.[6]

This was a very shocking story for a black person to write in a public newspaper, and the judge had Daisy and L.C. Bates arrested for printing a story that implied that the court was dishonest. Daisy went to jail! Luckily, her lawyer petitioned a different judge, who ruled that she couldn't be put in jail for expressing her opinion. Daisy got out seven hours later. It was stories such as this one that made the *State Press* famous and made it a leading voice for the Civil Rights movement.

Chapter 6

Days of Change

I n the early 1940s, Daisy Bates gathered momentum like a huge magnet sweeping across Little Rock, picking up civil rights causes and activities everywhere she went. She joined over two dozen civil rights and religious organizations. Between her involvement in all these organizations and the growing popularity of the *State Press,* Daisy and L.C. became famous in their community and beyond. They had many friends and were seen as leaders of the black community.

In spite of these commitments, Daisy decided to go back to school and enrolled at Shorter College, one of the few colleges in the Little Rock area that was open to black people at the time. She took classes in business administration and public relations. She also fulfilled a lifelong dream and learned to fly an airplane. Much to her disappointment, though, she never got her license. In America in those days, it was unusual for women–and almost unheard of for black women–to learn how to fly. Insurance companies presumed that black women were a much greater risk flying an airplane than white men were, so insurance for them was extremely expensive. Daisy couldn't afford the insurance, so she had to stop flying.

Daisy's visibility in Little Rock made her the perfect candidate to provide the young, fresh leadership that the NAACP anticipated would be necessary as the Civil Rights movement picked up steam. The head of the local branch of the NAACP visited Daisy one day at the paper and asked her if she would be interested in working for the NAACP. In 1952, she became the president of the Arkansas Conference of the NAACP chapters.

Daisy believed that children were the hope of the future, so one of the first things she did in her new position at the NAACP was to organize a youth council in Little Rock. "We'd meet downstairs in the rec room, once a week for two hours. There were about 100 of them," said Daisy. "For the first hour we had to have a serious discussion on some major issue and the next hour they could dance and have fun."[1] The youth council was unusual, because most youth organizations in those days were primarily for white children.

No one knew it at the time, but this youth council, and Daisy's relationship with some of the children in it, laid the groundwork for what would become one of the defining events of the Civil Rights movement in America. The tie that linked Daisy's youth council to the Civil Rights movement was a court case about segregated schools, which had slowly made its way to the Supreme Court of the United States. The case, represented by a brilliant African American lawyer from the NAACP named Thurgood Marshall, was called *Brown v. the Topeka Board of Education*. This case would completely change Daisy's life, and would alter the course of history forever in the United States. It is often referred to as the most important Supreme Court case of the twentieth century. Many people consider it the catalyst for the Civil Rights movement, because it marked the beginning of the end of racial segregation in America.

The case started when the father of Linda Brown, a seven-year-old girl from Topeka, Kansas, tried to enroll his daughter in the public summer school program, and she was denied because she was black. Mr. Brown called the NAACP, which took the case, along with several other Topeka plaintiffs who were upset about the same issue.

Mr. Brown and the NAACP lost the first round in this case based on a precedent that had been set in 1896, called *Plessy v. Fergusson.* The *Plessy* case had also argued the unfairness of segregation, but then the court had ruled that as long as the facilities—in the *Plessy* case, railroad cars—were equal, the races could be separated. The *Plessy v. Fergusson* case had been used to justify segregation ever since.

The NAACP appealed the decision on the *Brown* case, and while they lost in appeals court as well, a significant idea was presented in that appeal which led to the ultimate victory over the "separate but equal" doctrine. This idea was that, in effect, the rationale for "separate but equal" was an oxymoron—a contradiction of itself. By the time the case reached the United States Supreme Court, Thurgood Marshall had honed his case to a sharp, clear point: He argued that the reason for separating the races in the first place—the widely held belief that white people were superior to black people—was what *caused* inequality. He argued that "separate" was inherently, or naturally, unequal. And he argued that legal endorsement of this attitude further damaged black children's motivation and ability to learn.

The Supreme Court unanimously agreed with that argument, and on May 17, 1954, Justice Earl Warren effectively reversed the *Plessy v. Fergusson* decision, stating in part, "Does segregation of children in public schools solely on the basis of race, even though the physical facilities and other 'tangible' factors may be equal, deprive the children of the minority group of equal educational opportunities? We believe that it does. We conclude that in the field of public education, the doctrine of 'separate but equal' has no place."[2]

The decision was a big shock to most Americans. It appeared to many white people that this decision, and the Civil Rights movement, came like a lightning storm out of the clear blue sky. They were stunned. Segregation had been an accepted practice for many years in the United States, and now it was suddenly illegal. Even Daisy, who had worked hard toward achieving civil rights for blacks, was amazed. It never occurred to her that the fight for civil rights would become so intense and visible in her lifetime.

Some people rejoiced and considered the *Brown* decision a great victory for America. But many people were afraid. They wanted more time to get used to the idea. These people, both black and white, feared that this decision would stir things up and cause more violence between the two races. Most people, regardless of how they felt, were willing to go along with whatever the law said. There was, however, a sizable and vocal minority of people, both black and white, who were not ready to cooperate with integration and were willing to fight about it. Many southerners said, "We don't care what the Supreme Court says, we're not doing it!"[3]

Daisy and other members of the NAACP were ecstatic about the *Brown* decision. Finally, all their hard work to expose and eliminate racism was about to pay off. Integrated schools would be a tremendous step forward. Questions burned in their minds: When? How? What can we do to help? Because while the Supreme Court justices had said that segregation must end, they said nothing about how this would happen, or how long it would take.

At first things looked promising in Little Rock. The governor of Arkansas, Francis A. Cherry, replied right away to the decision: "Arkansas [will] obey the law."[4] In fact, only one week after the *Brown* decision was announced to the nation, the Little Rock School Board voted unanimously to adopt the superintendent's plan of gradual integration that would start in September, 1957. Superintendent Virgil Blossom had been working on the plan even before the Brown decision was made, and he was named "Man of the Year" by the local Arkansas newspaper for his work on desegregation that year. But shortly after this announcement, a man named Orval Faubus took office as the new governor of Arkansas, in January, 1955. In his campaign he had promised that if he were elected, integration would not happen until people felt more ready for it. After his election, Daisy's joy over the *Brown* decision turned to disappointment as it became clear that, indeed, Mr. Faubus intended to delay integration for as long as he possibly could.

Once Governor Faubus was in control, people who didn't want integration to occur became more vocal. Superintendent Blossom responded to these people by putting the brakes on the leisurely integration timeline he had just created. Now, instead of integrating all of Little Rock's high schools at the same time, as was originally planned, he said he would integrate the high schools one at a time. Central High School was to be the first.

Daisy and the others in the NAACP tried to be patient, but they had been tracking the plans for the desegregation of the Little Rock schools for two years already since the *Brown* decision. They had witnessed other nearby school districts that had accommodated integration with little fuss, only months after the *Brown* decision was made. Daisy didn't think the Blossom plan was so great *before* he rescinded his initial intentions. And now the initial number of 200 or so black students slated to attend Central High School in the fall of 1957 had been pared steadily down, with mounting pressure from segregationist factions to reduce it to nothing.

By the spring of 1956, Daisy—who was tired of waiting—rounded up thirty-three African Americans in Little Rock to go to court with NAACP lawyers to try and speed up the process of integration. This was a very courageous thing to do. Many powerful white people were ready and willing to destroy anyone who threatened what they saw as their right to segregation. It was dangerous for Daisy and others to publicly push for integration.

The court didn't agree to speed up the integration process, but Judge John Miller did order the school board to stick to its promise to follow through with the first phase of the integration plan in September of 1957.

While Daisy and the NAACP were in court, the politicians in the Arkansas state government were also in session, creating new laws to slow integration down. They introduced four new "Jim Crow" (a slang term to indicate discrimination against blacks) laws that would allow the Arkansas government to override any orders by the federal government that it felt was unfair. These new laws were very controversial, so the Arkansas Senate held a public meeting to listen to what Little Rock citizens wanted. About 900 people, both black and white, showed up at the meeting. Although this only represented a small fraction of the population, it was still one of the largest public demonstrations in Little Rock's history. All the people who attended in support of integration–the majority–were at great risk of being ostracized in their community, or even harmed, for doing so.

Those at the meeting who favored segregation argued that the U. S. Supreme Court shouldn't have the last word if it was going to uproot customs that people had adhered to for well over a hundred years. The people in favor of integration spoke about how the proposed laws would violate God's commandments to "love your neighbor," as well as disobey the orders of the highest court in the United States, and that was a moral and legal crime. Even though hundreds of citizens in Little Rock came to the hearing to protest the laws that the politicians had created, the laws were passed, thus setting the stage for the riots that would follow in the coming months.

Armed with the new Jim Crow laws as additional weapons to fight integration, segregationists from Little Rock and other southern states rallied their forces. The battle built up steam all summer long. Daisy and the NAACP faced quite a bit of opposition from both the black and the white communities. After all, Superintendent Blossom had begun work on his integration plan even before the *Brown* decision was handed down. Its glacial pace didn't really bother most of the community, which was accustomed to segregation anyway, and feared the conflict that integration might churn up.

The turmoil was pretty much confined to Little Rock and its immediate southern neighbors at this point, but in these areas, Daisy's work toward integration earned her a reputation as the troublemaker. She and L.C. bore the brunt of the anger and fear people felt about the changes they were being asked to make. As the summer of 1957 neared an end and the first day of school approached, strangers began calling her house and sending threatening letters. Carloads of Ku Klux Klansmen circled her house each night, shouting insults and threats, and throwing things at the house. Throughout all of this, Daisy and L.C. were surprisingly calm and collected. They knew what had to be done and believed that everything would come out all right.

The first thing Daisy had done once the court ruled that Central High must be integrated that fall was to talk to black families within the district to see who would be willing to consider transferring their children from an all-black school to Central High School. Daisy found 215 interested students, and they attended a meeting with Superintendent Virgil Blossom to learn about what it would be like to transfer to the new school. After the meeting, two thirds of the students decided that they didn't want to go after all. This was exactly the kind of thing that made Daisy distrust Blossom's motives in the first place. While he publicly claimed that he supported and would comply with integration efforts, his actions always seemed to thwart them. Daisy was convinced that Blossom's true plan was to admit as few black students to as few white schools as he could get away with and still keep the federal government off his back. Southern state government officials had been at odds with the federal government as far back as the Civil War. They really believed that individual states should have the right to govern themselves without interference, but when push came to shove, they weren't willing to butt heads with the federal government. Daisy accused Blossom of intentionally scaring black families so much that they would elect not to transfer their children to Central High School.

In the end, Superintendent Blossom *did* make a token selection of only seventeen students to attend Central High School, and eight of them backed out before school even started. The nine remaining students were all members of Daisy's youth council. Ernest Green, Elizabeth Eckford, Jefferson Thomas, Terrence Roberts, Carlotta Walls, Minnijean Brown, Gloria Ray, Thelma Mothershed, and Melba Pattillo were different ages and had different interests, but they had much in common. They were all good students from strict, stable home environments. They were all involved in the church, had strong opinions, and were proud of who they were. Their parents had high expectations for them. And they were all determined to go to school at Central High, where the opportunities for a good education were so much greater than at their all-black high school.

Now, in the last summer months before the nine students were expected to go to Central High School, Daisy spent every day working hard to prepare them for the challenge. She helped them with everything, from registering at the new school to getting their books and selecting their clothes, to learning how to handle themselves in difficult situations.

As the first day of school neared, the fear of integration that infected most of the Little Rock community seeped up to the surface and Daisy began to see more clearly the magnitude of the difficulties she and the students, now known as the "Little Rock Nine," were about to face. The segregationists in Little Rock scrambled desperately to avoid integration in any way they could.

Chapter 7

Tension Builds in Little Rock

Daisy knew that peaceful integration would be a tremendous challenge. She was very concerned about how her nine dark-skinned envoys would cope among the 1,200 white students at Central High School. Before they even set foot in the school, the superintendent told the new students that they would not be allowed to participate in athletics or clubs because they were transfer students. No one believed this was the reason.

Maturity was a major consideration in the selection of black students who would attend Central High, because it was anticipated that some degree of harassment would be unavoidable. They could expect to be teased and taunted, pushed around, and completely excluded from the social lives of the other students. People might spit or throw things at them, push them down the stairs, or knock the books from their arms. Daisy knew that her students would be strictly forbidden to fight or talk back to the white students who might harass them. If they retaliated in any way, then they would be disciplined along with their attackers. No matter how bad it was, these nine young people would have to understand that they must either ignore all instances of harassment or report them to the school authorities. The Little Rock Nine would have to be far more mature and patient than most adults. Daisy was determined to see to it that they succeeded at Central High School.

Daisy Bates anticipated the anger her students would feel; she remembered it well from her own childhood. Now Daisy used all the things she had learned about creating something positive out of her own anger to teach them how to do the same thing. Besides L.C., two people who had really inspired Daisy to focus her anger into productive change were Martin Luther King, Jr. in America and Mahatma Gandhi in India. These men both became very famous for their success in changing societal wrongs through passive resistance. They believed that the only outcome of hate and violence was more hate and violence; that education, understanding and economic pressure through boycotts were the keys to eliminating racism. They organized large groups of calm, orderly protestors, but those who opposed them reacted violently. The media widely covered these new, peaceful protests, which made the opposition look like bullies. In this way, the authorities in question were pressured to change their policies.

Daisy's instructions to her students if they encountered racist or even violent treatment from other students were based on what she had learned from the teachings of these two men. She coached the children to hold their heads high, look ahead, breathe deeply, and keep calm at all times. She reminded them that the whole world would be watching them, and it was imperative that they set an example that would leave no doubt that integration was the right course of action. "Be strong and keep your dignity. I know you can do it,"[1] she counseled.

While Daisy prepared the students for their new environment, the community continued to pressure her to cease her efforts for integration. Eleven days before school was to start, Daisy tasted for the first time the fear and chaos that were about to take over her life. She was watching the eleven o'clock news on television, where there were about three hundred people cheering at a local rally to fight integration. Disgusted, Daisy took her little dog, Skippy, out for his nightly walk. She was sitting on a sofa after she returned when a large rock came crashing through the living room window behind her. Daisy dove to the floor for cover, and her husband, L.C., found her there, covered with broken glass. Daisy was very lucky that she didn't get hurt. Neatly tied around that rock was a little slip of paper that carried a message of hate which kept her up all night long: "STONE THIS TIME. DYNAMITE NEXT!"[2]

The segregationists were now desperate to prevent integration. Just four days after the rock incident, a group of white women from Little Rock who called themselves the Mothers League went to court to ask for a delay in the process. They claimed that they knew many students, both black and white, had purchased guns and knives to bring to school, and they petitioned the court to halt integration in order to protect all the students. Governor Faubus testified at this court hearing that he agreed with the Mothers League. Integration, he said, posed a danger at this time and should be postponed until the people of Little Rock were better prepared for it. The judge granted the delay order. That night, carloads of people drove up and down Daisy's street, honking and screaming with glee, "Daisy. Daisy. The coons won't be going to Central!"[3]

The FBI and dozens of reporters searched all the records of local stores to verify the story about the weapons, but could find nothing that supported it. The NAACP appealed the decision to Judge Ronald N. Davies, who ruled that there was no evidence that dangerous weapons would be a problem in Central High School; that integration was to proceed immediately; and that no one was to interfere with it for any reason. This was just three days before the first day of school, and segregationists, emboldened by the near-success of the Mothers League and by the hysteria that gripped their community, pleaded, ranted, and rioted in the streets to prevent school integration from occurring.

On Monday, September 2, the day before school was to begin, a news reporter from Little Rock knocked at Daisy's door after dinner. "Mrs. Bates, do you know that national guardsmen are surrounding Central High School?"[4] he asked excitedly. Daisy and L.C. were incredulous. They wanted to see this for themselves, but ever since the rock had shattered their window they felt that their lives and their home were in constant danger. They had been provided token protection from the local police force, but they also felt the need to take security measures of their own. L.C. handed over his guns and the responsibility for protecting their home to a neighbor so they could leave.

When Daisy and L.C. arrived at the school, they saw hundreds of guardsmen in full battle dress, rifles in hand, planted around Central High School in a thick circle. When Daisy asked them why they were there, they looked straight ahead with steely eyes and were silent. She had heard that Governor Faubus was going to make an announcement on television that night and, seeing that she was being stonewalled by the guardsmen, Daisy and L.C. raced back home to hear the speech.

At ten o'clock that night, in the space of a few short minutes, Governor Faubus delivered a speech that instantly toppled the teetering Little Rock into chaos. He explained that he had called the National Guard—a state level protection unit—out in order to prevent violence at Central High School. When later asked why he chose the National Guard rather than the local police to enforce protection, Faubus claimed that police forces were insufficient to deal with the magnitude of expected upheaval. When Little Rock mayor Woodrow Mann was questioned, however, he had a different story. He said "The governor has called out the National Guard to put down trouble when none existed."[5]

In his speech, Governor Faubus said he had heard from unnamed sources that carloads of people from all over the state were heading

The Little Rock Nine and Daisy Bates. Seated, from left: Thelma Mothershed, Minnijean Brown, Elizabeth Eckford, Gloria Ray. Standing, from left, Ernest Green, Melba Pattillo, Jefferson Thomas, Carlotta Walls, Daisy Bates, Terrence Roberts. *Courtesy of the National Association for the Advancement of Colored People (NAACP) at the Library of Congress.*

The Ku Klux Klan often burned crosses like this as a signature of their presence, to threaten and intimidate African Americans like Daisy Bates who "stepped out of line." *Photo by Larry Obsitnik by permission of the Arkansas Democrat-Gazette. Daisy Bates Papers (MC 582), Series 4, Subseries 16, Box 11, #443. Special Collections, University of Arkansas Libraries, Fayetteville.*

Top right: Weariness and trepidation mark the faces of Daisy and L.C. Bates as they watch Arkansas Governor Orval Faubus on television. *Photo by International News Photos. Courtesy of the Wisconsin Historical Society, Daisy Bates Collection, Image # Whi-5003.*

Bottom right: White citizens marched and rioted in the streets of Little Rock in an attempt to prevent the integration of Central High School. *Courtesy of the Arkansas Democrat-Gazette.*

Threats and Intimidations Won't Keep Negroes Out of Federal Courts Says Thurgood Marshall

—See Story page Fifteen

Americanism Award Goes to The Nine Central High School Negroes

Responses from an estimated audience, of some 1400 people, Little Rock was host to one of the most spectacular meetings the city has ever held, Sunday at Bethel AME church when the Little Rock Nine was given the "Americanism Award."

Representative groups from every section of the state, and many parts of the nation, were on hand to witness the Nine Negro children who have braved the hate of a certain element of Arkansas to advance their education at Central hi school.

The Award was given by the American Veterans Committee and presented in person to the Nine by Chat Paterson Cleveland Ohio industralist and chairman of the Americanism Committee of the AVC.

Paterson's presentation of the Award, followed one of the most eloquent addresses heard in many years, by the eminent attorney of Chicago, William R. Ming jr. president of American Veterans Committee.

The noted barrister was introduced to the audience by Wiley Branton, Pine Bluff businessman

and attorney.

A brief history of the Veterans' organization, which is thoroughly integrated was given by Dr. J. B. Woods.

Others appearing on program were the Rev. J. C. Crenchaw, Rev. C. D. Alstork. sr., Rev. Rufus K. Young who made the welcome address. Horace Mann hi school choir, under the direction of Frederick J. Rasdon, furnished music for the occasion with Misses Francis Smith and Continued on page Three—

Continued on page Three—

VOLUME 17—NUMBER 39   FRIDAY, JANUARY 31, 1958   LITTLE ROCK, ARKANSAS   PRICE TEN CENTS

Little Rock Nine Gets $1,000 Aid to Scholarship Fund

Checks of $1000 each were presented to the National Association for the Advancement of Colored People and the Scholarship Fund for the nine Negro students at the recently integrated Central high school at Little Rock, by the Amalgamated Machine Instrument and Metal Local Union 461, IUE, AFL-CIO.

Receiving the contributions at the local's annual conference here at Manhattan Center on Jan. 22 were Roy Wilkins, executive secretary, NAACP, and Clarence A. Laws, field secretary, assigned to work in Little Rock with Mrs. L. C. Bates, Arkansas State NAACP president.

Mr. Wilkins commended the labor organization on its continuing effort for human betterment and understanding and said that working with organized labor was

"one of the Association's most cherished traditions."

Continuing difficulty at the Little Rock high school was reported by Mr. Laws who listed the following reasons for the worsening situation:

1. Continuing agitation by Governor Orval Faubus and other politicians;
2. Failure of federal and local law enforcement agencies to prosecute persons involved in mob violence at the school in September;
3. Failure of school officials to enunciate a firm, positive policy to cope with racial incidents; and
4. Failure of so-called responsible citizens to take a strong stand for law and order in Little Rock.

RECEIVE "AMERICANISM AWARD"—This foto was taken following one of the most spectacular meetings held in Little Rock in recent years, when the nine children attending Central hi school, were given the "Americanism Award" by the American Veterans Committee. The award was made Sunday at Bethel AME church.

Back row standing l. to r. Mrs. L. C.

Bates, State President NAACP; Chat Paterson, Chairman, Americanism Comit., AVC; Thelma Mothershed, and Willie Ming, Jr., National Chairman of AVC.

Front row l. to r. Melba Pattilla, Earnest Green, Thomas Jefferson, Elizabeth Ann Eckford, Gloria Ray, Minnie jean Brown, Terrance Roberts and Carlotta Walls.   —Foto by Davy

Mississippi Posse Slaying Called A "Legal Lynching" by Naacp Officer

important announcement —Page Sixteen

—Page Sixteen

In Meet at Community Center Pulaski County Mothers Prepare to March for Funds to Fight Polio

—Page Nine

Elks Launch $100,000.00 Scholarship Drive at Banquet in Philadelphia Tonite —Mrs. Bates Honored

—See story page sixteen

to Little Rock to stop the integration. On national television he asked the Little Rock Nine not to come to school the next day. He said that he feared that blood would run in the streets if they did.

Daisy was stunned, as were many, many people in Little Rock. By the next day, so was most of the United States. What was Faubus saying? He knew that the highest court in the United States had ordered a stop to segregation. Little Rock had been repeatedly told that it must proceed with integration at Central High School in September. Were those troops there to defy the orders of the Supreme Court of the United States?

Daisy leapt into action. She conferred with others in the NAACP. They couldn't risk the children's safety under these circumstances, and instructed the black students not to go to school the next day, until Daisy and the other NAACP officials received assurance that they would be safe. On September 3, instead of overseeing the Little Rock Nine's first day of school as planned, Daisy kept in close contact with their families while the NAACP attorneys went to see Judge Davies to ask him what to do. Judge Davies reassured them that Governor Faubus must have put the National Guard there to protect the students, since that was the law of the land. He instructed the Little Rock Nine to attend school on the 4th. Daisy called all the families to relay the message. Then Superintendent Blossom called together a meeting of the Little Rock Nine families. Daisy went along, even though she wasn't invited. She felt personally responsible for the safety of those nine children.

At the meeting, the superintendent instructed the children to come to school without their parents. He thought this would make it easier to protect them. Daisy thought the parents looked very nerv-

---

The masthead of the *State Press* was drawn by L.C. himself. When Daisy first asked L.C. what it meant, he said simply, "That's me!" *Courtesy of Arkansas Council on Human Relations Box 19, File 188. Special Collections, University of Arkansas Libraries, Fayetteville.*

ous about this plan, and she was too. She pictured the nine young-sters walking through hundreds or thousands of angry protesters into a school of 1,200 white students, most of whom didn't want them there. Daisy was uneasy with this arrangement; all the rest of that day and night she worried about it.

Finally, late that night, she came up with what she thought was the perfect idea. She called several local ministers, both black and white, and asked them to escort the children to school. Surely, no one would dare cause trouble with these respected religious men leading the way. But many of the ministers were too frightened to help. Daisy spent most of the night calling all the ministers she knew to find a few who were brave enough to help, and conferring with police to select a safe place so the ministers and students could meet before entering the school as a protected block. She even thought about exactly how the ministers would position themselves among the students and which door they would approach to enter the school. Then she called all the families of the Little Rock Nine to let them know where to meet the next morning so they would be together and protected when they reached the school. There was one student, Elizabeth Eckford, who didn't have a telephone, so Daisy made a mental note to go to Elizabeth's house immediately after she woke up. It was almost dawn when Daisy finally stumbled, exhausted, to bed.

After only a few hours of sleep, Daisy awoke to chaos. The phone rang constantly with reporters, and carloads of hostile people were honking up and down the street. Tuning it all out, Daisy was up and running again. As she and L.C. drove to the church where she had told everyone to meet, she went over all the details of the plan in her mind again. Suddenly a report on the radio jolted her into a panic about the one detail she had forgotten–Elizabeth! The reporter urgently described a single African American child being mobbed at Central High School. L.C. jumped out of the car and ran over to the school while Daisy, consumed with anguish and worry for Elizabeth, drove to the agreed-upon meeting place, one block away from the school and out of sight of the angry mob.

When Daisy arrived, almost everyone was there. Melba Patillo was the only other student who hadn't made it, because she and her mother had parked too far off and were chased away by the mob. Four ministers, two black and two white, were waiting at the designated corner with the other seven children and the police who had promised to come. Before the group started their walk to school, the radio reported that Elizabeth had gotten away to safety. The moment that had been carefully planned for months was now here. Proceeding with two ministers leading, two following, and the students sandwiched between, the group slowly walked with determination toward the mass of hate-filled people and the silent guard.

Chapter 8

Chaos in Little Rock

The students and the ministers slowly and purposefully walked into the thick of the crowd, and were met with eyes that beamed hatred at them. When they came up against the National Guard, the soldiers raised their rifles to bar the students' entrance. The crowd cheered in approval. Shouts of "Niggers, go home!"; "Two, four, six, eight, we ain't gonna integrate,"; and even demands for lynching rang out among the cheers.[1] One of the ministers asked a captain why they were not being let through. The captain replied that the Guard was acting on the governor's orders. The crowd closed in chanting, spitting, and throwing things as the little group made its way back to Daisy and the policemen on the street corner. The ministers' eyes blazed with anger.

Daisy knew that she had the law on her side. She drove the students straight to the office of Superintendent Blossom. When they got there, he was nowhere to be found. They sat and waited for an entire hour, but no one was able to locate him. Daisy moved on to the next level of authority.

Mr. Osro Cobb, a United States attorney who represented the federal government as chief law enforcement officer for the district, was surprised when Daisy and her group showed up at his office.

Evidently, he didn't know that the children had been sent away from school. After a few questions about what went wrong, he sent them to the office of the FBI, the Federal Bureau of Investigation, so a thorough investigation could be conducted. The students reported the details of their traumatic morning and the FBI officials took lots of notes. When they finished, the FBI said they'd investigate the matter and sent the students home. Daisy and her students were left with no protection, no school to attend, and no directions for what to do next.

The first thing Daisy decided to do was to find a way to teach the nine students what they were missing in their classes at Central High School. With help from a few people in Little Rock who were willing to publicly support integration, Daisy arranged for the use of a room in a local college. She had the children write letters to Superintendent Blossom requesting their books, assignments, and class schedules. Then she persuaded teachers from several local schools to offer to tutor the nine young people.

Meanwhile, the FBI investigated. For the next two weeks, while Daisy, the NAACP, and the federal courts and officers studied the situation, Little Rock became a bully's paradise. A few days after the Little Rock Nine were denied entrance to Central High School, an eight-foot-tall cross was burned on Daisy's lawn. It had a message attached that said, "Go back to Africa, signed the KKK."[2] Angry segregationists now called Daisy and L.C. and the children on the phone and threatened them. In low, menacing voices they said things like, "Nigger, I know where you live. We gonna get you tonight."[3] Then, click, they hung up. They made life-size cloth dolls, called effigies, that looked like the Little Rock Nine. They hung them in places outdoors and lit them on fire, then cheered as they watched the dolls burn. Daisy and the Little Rock Nine couldn't go anywhere in public without attracting huge crowds of angry white tormentors.

During the two weeks they waited for answers from the courts, the hardest part for Daisy Bates was the tremendous pressure on her to give up and stop pushing for integration. She received hundreds of letters and phone calls, from both black and white people, begging her to let things be and telling her she could never change them. Many of the letters said that America had always been and would always be segregated, and that she should accept the fact that black people weren't as good as white people. Many black and white Americans wrote to say that the separation of the races was God's will. Some people wrote and called on the phone threatening the lives and homes of the Bateses and the students.

Daisy was scared for her own safety, but she was more terrified for the safety of the Little Rock Nine and their families, who were like her own family. She and L.C. were exhausted from the stress of fighting what had become an all-out war for integration all day every day, and then sitting up all night in shifts, protecting their home and their lives.

Daisy thought many times about giving up, but in the end, she knew in her heart that integration was worth fighting for. She firmly believed that it would help advance other civil rights for Negroes. She received at least as many letters and telephone calls of praise as she did threats. People called and wrote from all over the world, congratulating her on her courage and perseverance, and thanking her for helping to make America a better country for everyone. These people talked about God, too. They said they thought Daisy must be a messenger from God because she was strong enough to fight this very difficult battle for justice. Some people told her in their letters that they were ashamed to be white because of what their race had done to black people. Many people sent her money to help with the struggle. The money was put in an account for post-high-school education of the Little Rock Nine. All the support that Daisy received from these strangers, her friends and family, and the families of the Little Rock Nine gave her the courage to continue the fight.

Finally, on September 20, 1957, Judge Ronald N. Davies responded. He ordered Governor Faubus to tell the National Guard that they could not keep the Little Rock Nine out of Central High School. Judge Davies told the new students that they were to attend Central High School on Monday morning, September 23.

Governor Faubus was very angry. On national television, he again made a speech urging the black students to stay away from school until things cooled down a bit. The governor repeated his warning that if the black students attended Central High School, he feared that local police would not be able to contain the violence that would occur. Faubus had the option of keeping the National Guard at Central High School to help the local police protect the black students. But instead, as if thumbing his nose at all the people who said he was blowing things out of proportion, Governor Faubus sent the troops away. Then he left town with his wife for a long weekend, washing his hands of the whole ordeal.

Little Rock was stricken in shocked silence. The most powerful businessmen in the city all gathered together to solve the problem. They wrote a resolution that they thought represented the majority view. The resolution stated that the people of Little Rock believed in law and order and the absence of violence. It was widely publicized and the businessmen urged all citizens to support it regardless of how they felt about integration. In eighty-four churches in Little Rock that weekend, people prayed for peace. While the resolution didn't openly condone integration, it begged the citizens of Little Rock to cooperate with the judge's order because it was the law.

Unfortunately, the attitudes and activities of the fierce segregationist minority rubbed off on enough people throughout the state of Arkansas to create havoc at Central High School on Monday morning. Some people believed that Faubus, while on his vacation with his wife, had helped to organize the mayhem that was to occur in order to prove his point that people weren't ready for integration.

Early that September 23 morning, the Little Rock Nine convened at Daisy's house. Phones rang, the radio and television blared, and reporters came and went, urging caution due to the mob of over a thousand segregationists hovering in a mass around the school. Throughout the commotion, the nine children sat silently with solemn expressions, waiting to go. Their faces showed determined pride as the radio announcers reported increasing numbers of segregationists building up in front of the school. Remarks from that crowd spilled into Daisy's living room from the radio and television. "They're not going to get in," one man threatened. "They won't live long enough to get through the doors."[4]

Finally, local policemen came in two cars to transport the children to school. They took roads that bypassed the crowd. As the children quietly slipped through a side entrance, the frenzied mob attacked a small group of black reporters in front of the school. The attackers did not care that these were reporters. The only thing that mattered was that they were black. The crowd descended on them, punching, kicking, spitting, and threatening. They smashed their cameras and were about to bludgeon one reporter with a brick when someone realized that the nine children were already in the school. "They're in! The niggers are in!"[5] was shouted into the crowd, and the man with the brick ran for the school.

All morning, the police managed to keep the savage mob out of the school, but no one inside was fooled. Even with the windows closed, the noise coming from the streets sounded like fans roaring at a sports event. The parents of the nine students were frantic with worry because they kept hearing reports on the radio that the children were being cornered and beaten. But Daisy was in contact all morning with the police officer in charge of protecting the students. He kept assuring her that the reports were false and she relayed this message to the worried parents. By noon, though, the crowd had become so large and menacing that Little Rock's mayor, Woodrow Wilson Mann, ordered the Little Rock Nine to be withdrawn for their safety. Though he guided them quickly and quietly out of the school through the kitchen entrance, the crowd found them. They battered the windshield of one of the escape cars and yelled obscenities as the two cars raced away.

That night, black homes were vandalized, black people were torn from their cars and beaten, and chanting mobs rioted in the streets. Policemen sat outside the homes of all the families of the Little Rock Nine and the Bateses to protect them. Daisy and L.C. were not allowed to leave. Around midnight, L.C. watched a police cruiser follow a suspicious-looking car outside their home. Minutes later, the policeman was back. Quickly, he turned off all the lights in the Bateses' house and instructed them to stay away from the window. He had followed the car to a caravan of about a hundred cars, only two blocks away, that were filled with people wielding guns, clubs, and enough dynamite to blow up the whole neighborhood. The policeman had radioed for help, then returned to the Bateses to warn them. "That's when I was most frightened," Daisy said later in an interview. "I didn't know if the police would or could stop them. They were coming to lynch us."[6]

The local police were enough to hold the mob away, but no one slept that night. At 2:30 A.M. Daisy received a call. The voice on the other end said, "We didn't get you last night but we will. And you better not try to put those coons in our school!"[7]

The next day Mayor Mann wired the President of the United States to request federal army assistance. At first reluctant to get involved, President Eisenhower, fed up with the situation, proclaimed on national television that all who were getting in the way of integration in Little Rock must cease their disruption immediately. "I will use my full power," he cautioned, "to see that the federal order is carried out."[8] Daisy called all the families of the Little Rock Nine to make sure they had enough protection. She told them not to go to school the next day, despite the president's televised speech. She didn't think that his warning would be enough to drive away the hostile mob of segregationists.

LETTERS TO LITTLE ROCK

New York City
Sept. 24, 1957

Dear Mrs. Bates:

I am a white Southerner now living in New York. After reading in todays New York Times of your courageous work in Little Rock, I am moved to let you know that I am proud of you and the Negroe people of Little Rock for your magnificent behavior in this dark hour of our country's history. Without you and others like you this would be an even darker hour indeed. This is just to let you know that you have the admiration of many outside of Little Rock who know that you are fighting the fight for all of us who believe in a more truly democratic America.

* * * * *

Nashville, Arkansas
September 23, 1957

Dear Mrs. Bates:

The members of the Nashville, Arkansas, Good Citizens League wish to commend and congratulate you for the gallant stand you have taken in the fight for integration in the Little Rock Schools. The Courage, spirit, and determination that you displayed throughout the past weeks is proof to the world of the great qualities you possess. May God be with you all the way in this fight against evil and hatred.

* * * * *

Jacksonville, Fla.,
September 24, 1957

Central High Mother's League
Little Rock, Arkansas

Dear Madam:

Times seems black for the white people of the South indeed, especially in view of the President's Action of Today.

However, I believe, the South still has its most potent weapon available that I have never seen advocated, and I am surprised that I have not. That is economic pressure. If the white people of the South would fire every negro who works for them a stop would soon be put to this business of integration. Then the negro would have to go North for a living where they claim to have so much interest in him but I think it is only for political advantage. Then see if the NAACP would support them. I do not believe the NAACP represents the thinking of the majority of the colored people. It certainly does not of those to whom I Have talked.

I do not believe this would be in violation of any law, and if it is I would not advocate it. But it seems that some drastic measures are going to have to be taken to put a stop to this business and I think this would be most effective.

I am just an inconsequential individual who likes to see the negro get ahead, have fine cars, fine homes and a good living as long as they keep to themselves, so will not sign my name as I cannot afford to become involved.[9]

Daisy was right. About five hundred angry protesters showed up the next morning to keep the black children out of school. When the Little Rock Nine didn't show up, the crowd slowly dispersed. President Eisenhower now had no choice but to respond to the defiant people in Little Rock.

That afternoon, Tuesday, September 24, 1957, President Eisenhower sent 1,000 troops from the 101st Airborne Infantry of the United States Army to Little Rock. He also ordered the same Arkansas National Guard that had prevented the black children from entering the school three weeks before to provide backup protection. That added 10,000 soldiers to preserving the peace in Little Rock and made the point that the president, and not Governor Faubus, was in charge.

On Wednesday morning, when the students prepared to leave Daisy's house to go to school, they were flanked on all sides by combat-ready soldiers. Each student was escorted from class to class by a personal guard, and soldiers waited at the doorway of each classroom that the African American students entered. Then, after school, they were driven back to Daisy's house surrounded by army jeeps full of soldiers.

There was a brief period of calm at the school. The soldiers made it clear that they would not tolerate harassment of any kind. A week later, when the federal army was withdrawn and the Arkansas National Guard was left to handle the situation, things quickly deteriorated. Central High School became a living nightmare for the nine black students.

Daisy and L.C. were left without protection once the army left. Their many friends united and organized to provide around-the-clock protection for their property and personal safety, but nothing could stop the segregationists from destroying other important parts of their lives.

Soon after the black students were escorted to school by the U.S. Army, a white woman visited Daisy at her home. She begged Daisy to do the "Christian thing" and convince the children to withdraw from Central High School. She promised that the Christian women of Little Rock would help prepare the community for integration if Daisy would give them some time. However, the woman would not give her any idea how much time it would take, so Daisy said no to the proposal. The woman then looked Daisy in the eye and said, "You'll be destroyed–you, your newspaper, your reputation. Everything!"[10]

The woman's threat was just the beginning. L.C. and Daisy's home literally became a battlefield, with constant streams of angry Little Rock citizens hurling insults and worse from passing cars. A second cross was placed up against the side of their house and ignited, nearly burning the house down. One of the Bateses' greatest losses was their foster son, a little boy named Clyde. Daisy and L.C. had been unable to have children of their own, and had cared for Clyde for six years when he was removed from their home for his safety. Daisy and L.C. were devastated to lose him.

For the next year, Daisy skillfully juggled all her commitments. In addition to her responsibilities at the *State Press* and in several other organizations and committees, she read thousands of letters of support and criticism, and she responded to almost every one of them. Daisy was the foremost African American representative in Little Rock and, because of this, she was hounded day and night by reporters and groups wanting information and speeches from her. Segregationists tried to wear Daisy down and distract her by having her arrested and taken to court for senseless reasons. Arkansas politicians were targeting Daisy personally when they created a law in the heat of the integration effort in 1957 that required the NAACP to publicize the names of all its members. As president of the Arkansas Conference of the NAACP chapters, Daisy would have to supply these names, but she knew that many NAACP members would drop out rather than run the risk of having their names available to segregationists. Daisy refused to give the names to the state government, and was initially arrested and thrown in jail for this refusal. NAACP lawyers got her out on bail, and the case went all the way to the United States Supreme Court. Once again, Daisy had the law on her side, and won, but it took three years of legal skirmishing to accomplish this, and it was used as another ploy to stall integration and "put her in her place."

Daisy's biggest responsibility, of course, was the welfare and success of the Little Rock Nine, whom she either met or talked with on the phone almost every day. She kept detailed records of every offense against the students and followed up with school officials to make sure these incidents were addressed. She arranged for help with their homework when they needed it, lifted their spirits by sharing the hundreds of letters of admiration she received, and coached them for interviews with reporters. She also got businesses to donate clothing and local beauticians to donate their services so the children would look their best during interviews.

Daisy enlisted the help of supportive people in the school to be her eyes and ears so she could intercept group attacks on the children when they were still in the planning stages. One time, a secret informant reported to her that the guards assigned to protect the Little Rock Nine had been instructed to do nothing but watch if other students ganged up on one of the students. Daisy happened to be in Washington D.C. when she heard this and she immediately hopped in a cab, walked into the Pentagon unannounced, and demanded action. Another time, the Little Rock Nine were about give up the fight and leave school. Daisy visited and called every local, state and national authority she knew, from Virgil Blossom to Thurgood Marshall to Val J. Washington, the director of the minorities division of the Republican National Committee in Washington, D.C. Within twenty-four hours, two soldiers from the 101st Airborne were at the sides of each of the black students in Central High.

One of the most important things Daisy did for the Little Rock Nine was to keep them focused. When they were weary and discouraged, Daisy reminded them that the world was watching them. She told them that how they handled this experience would have a significant impact on integration efforts across all of the United States.

Despite Daisy's best efforts, and those of many school personnel, the Little Rock Nine suffered terribly that year. The school grounds became a battlefield for them. They endured the daily routine of taunting and harassment without being able to retaliate, and the torment continued to escalate. At one point they were even threatened by white students wielding squirt guns filled with acid.

They couldn't escape the assault at home, either. The families of the Little Rock Nine, and Daisy and her husband, were in constant danger everywhere they went.

Chapter 9

Ripples from Little Rock

Most of the world lost interest in the problems of Little Rock once the excitement of armed troops and screaming mobs faded from the front pages of newspapers. Little Rock's struggles, however, had added to a growing controversy throughout the United States over integration. The *Brown* decision involved integrating schools, but it wasn't only about schools. Now, not only would black children and white children sit next to each other in class, but African Americans would share seats with Caucasians on buses; people of different color would stand in the same line as they shopped at the same stores; they would sit next to each other in theaters; and they would eat off the same dishes at the same restaurants. These were very radical ideas in much of the South at the time.

Particularly throughout the South, but in other places as well, African Americans began to demand their rights in all public places. Many white people responded with defiance. When African Americans seated themselves at previously all-white restaurants, some waitresses refused to serve them. Other white onlookers dumped soup on their heads, put cigarettes out on their skin, and knocked them off their seats. Segregationists bombed buses and churches full of people who were organizing to defend civil rights for

African Americans. City policemen broke up peaceful marches for civil rights with clubs and tear gas. Using the technique of passive resistance, the civil rights activists took the abuse, or allowed themselves to be arrested.

Little Rock was old news now that these incidents were erupting in other places, but whether they were covered on the news or not, the problems in Little Rock were far from over. Ernest Green was the first African American student to graduate from Central High School on May 27, 1958, and the ceremony took place without a hitch, but not because everyone had come to peace with integration. Even as Ernest walked across the stage to accept his diploma, a request from the Little Rock School Board sat with Judge Lemley–the judge who had once before attempted to stall integration–to interrupt the integration effort for a few years, until the community felt more comfortable with the idea. The school board insisted that they needed time to educate the public–that you couldn't legislate love. Daisy Bates had a response:

> We are not asking for love. We are *demanding* the rights and privileges as guaranteed under the Constitution of the United States–the right to move in a free society as free Americans. It is the duty of the highest federal official down to the constable in the smallest town in Arkansas or Mississippi to protect these rights.[1]

Judge Lemley agreed that integration was a constitutional right of black students, but warned that the "time has not come for them to enjoy that right."[2] His decision was to grant the request to delay integration indefinitely, beginning with the upcoming school year.

The NAACP immediately appealed the decision, and many people in Little Rock reacted with increased hostility, especially toward Daisy. She was accused by the governor and other important people of being power-hungry, too aggressive, and too outspoken. Daisy was flamboyant, and she lacked humility. She was proud, and in the opinions of many, overly dramatic. People claimed that she created all this commotion merely so she could be famous. Even many black leaders in the community shunned her. "She was too hot, so everybody steered clear,"[3] remarked a sociology professor who was familiar with the events in Little Rock.

When Daisy was seen walking down the street in Little Rock people booed and hissed, shouted threats, and pointed at her, calling out, "That's nigger Daisy."[4] She received several hundred letters a month, many of them hate mail and threats. One envelope contained nothing but three empty bullet shells. There were so many violent attacks on their home that Daisy and L.C. finally took out the shattered front picture window, boarded it up, and placed steel bars on all the windows of the house.

Though Daisy hated guns and violence, she learned how to use a gun to protect herself and her home from the constant attacks. Once when she was awakened by the thud of rocks raining down on her roof during this period, she snapped. Grabbing a loaded gun, she raced to the front door and fired a round of shots over the head of one of the boys milling outside her house. Then she broke down sobbing. "God help those hoodlums,"[5] she cried. She spent the rest of the night praying for forgiveness for her momentary loss of control.

Meanwhile, the appeal of the decision to delay integration in Little Rock went all the way to the Supreme Court of the United States. On August 25, 1958, the Supreme Court confirmed once again that the city must continue with integration in that fall.

Governor Faubus had suspected that the Supreme Court would vote in favor of integration and he was prepared. All during the summer of 1958, he and the Arkansas State Legislature had been busy creating new laws to get around that expected decision. When the Supreme Court ruling came, Governor Faubus closed all the high schools in Little Rock, on the basis of a new law that authorized the governor to close indefinitely any schools he deemed to be hazardous.

The town was thrown into an uproar once again. Within four days of the Supreme Court's decision, the citizens of Little Rock had splintered into squabbling forces. One dominant group called the Women's Emergency Committee to Re-open the Schools (WEC) consisted largely of the wives of well-educated and highly esteemed white professionals in the community. Because of who they were, because they appealed to black and white citizens alike for cooperation, and because their only request was for peaceful re-opening of the schools, they were influential with many citizens who were not hardcore segregationists. Another powerful group, the Committee to Retain Our Segregated Schools (CROSS), exerted equal pressure to keep the schools closed until the federal government agreed to allow them to remain segregated. The schools remained closed for the rest of the 1958-59 school year while the citizens of Little Rock remained deadlocked and in grave distress.

Although Daisy was scorned and hated in most of Little Rock, she and the Little Rock Nine were widely supported and admired by the rest of the world. During the summer of 1958, they all took a celebration trip to Cleveland, Ohio. Here, to the wild applause of a large audience, they received the first of many awards for their heroic struggle. The Spingarn Medal was a gold medal given by the NAACP each year to celebrate and reward extraordinary achievements of African Americans. Daisy and the Little Rock Nine were awarded this medal for their "pioneer role in upholding the basic ideals of American democracy in the face of continuing harassment and constant threats of bodily injury."[6] Martin Luther King, Jr. had received the Spingarn Medal the previous year.

While Daisy was the one who was caught in the crosshairs of Little Rock's anger, virtually everyone who had anything to do with the efforts at integration was affected. Several parents of the Little Rock Nine lost their jobs. Four of the nine families moved away from Little Rock to escape the constant abuse they received. The families that were left felt so beaten by the struggle that Daisy spent much of that year initiating a search for new black families who were willing to fight for their rights despite the terror they had now seen firsthand. Reverend Dunbar Ogden, who had accompanied the children on their first day at Central High School, was forced to resign from his church and move to another town. Several people, both black and white, gave in to despair and, consumed by hate and fear, hurt themselves or others. Daisy deeply mourned these losses and worried that one day she would be the one driven out or even killed.

When a dynamite bomb was thrown into Daisy's front yard a year later, blasting a hole in her lawn and reverberating throughout the entire neighborhood, she wrote a telegram to President Eisenhower requesting his assistance in protecting her. He responded that it was the job of local authorities to protect her. However, the local authorities, who were white, felt no loyalty to Daisy Bates. Later that summer, Arkansas state police arrested three of her volunteer security guards and kept them in jail all night. One of the victims, who was given no reason for his arrest, told Daisy the arresting officer's comment to his comrades: "We made a good haul tonight. . . . We got all of Daisy Bates' guards."[7]

Her life was now in such danger that very few people knew where Daisy would be at any given time. She was so traumatized that she had nightmares for nearly five years afterward. It also caused serious trouble in her marriage. Daisy and L.C. divorced for two years due to the strains of their long separations and the relentless stress and chaos.

In 1959, Daisy and L.C. lost the *State Press* as a direct result of their work for integration. The woman who had warned Daisy two years before that she would lose everything if she continued to push for integration, was right. Within weeks of that warning, many of the largest advertisers in the *State Press* had withdrawn their business and boycotted the paper. Daisy and L.C. received hundreds of letters of support, many of them with money enclosed, to help them maintain the paper during the boycott. Because of this aid, they were able to hang onto their paper for two whole years after the boycott began. But it wasn't enough. On October 29, 1959, at five o'clock, the last issue of the *State Press* was printed. Daisy was devastated. "The door was closed on the *State Press* and on eighteen years of our lives. No last good-byes, no final editorials," she said. "The break had to be clean and sharp, for the pain was too deep."[8]

A year after they were forced to close the *Press*, Daisy and L.C. joined a sit-in at the lunch counter in a Woolworth's five-and-dime store in Little Rock. This was a popular method of peaceful protest in the 1960s. Civil rights activists would take up all the seats in restaurants that still had segregated seating. They knew they wouldn't get served, and that they ran the chance of being arrested as well, but they were making a point while preventing the restaurant from serving anybody else.

The point they were making was that segregation was illegal, immoral, and unacceptable. To Daisy, six years of fighting what felt like a war for civil rights following the *Brown* decision had made her weary and disillusioned. In December, she was at the Capitol building in Washington D.C. with a friend who had been driven out of Little Rock because he had publicly supported integration. She saw some foreign students looking with admiration at the domed building and stifled an impulse to erase the stars from their eyes. She wanted to shout at them, "If all the victims of lynch mobs, if all the persons murdered in and out of court by Jim Crow [laws], if all the students beaten and jailed for simply trying to buy a cup of coffee or a Coke in America, if all of them were stacked like cordwood around the Capitol, you couldn't see that gorgeous building!"[9]

Needing another source of income, L.C. took a job as Arkansas field director of the NAACP. Daisy's life continued to be a hectic schedule of receiving awards, and speaking about civil rights and the ordeal of the Little Rock Nine. She based herself in New York during this time, where she started writing a book about her life and her experiences with the Little Rock Nine. Published in 1962, *The Long Shadow of Little Rock* had a foreword by former first lady Eleanor Roosevelt.

Speaking tours took Daisy around the world, and linked her not only with Eleanor Roosevelt, but also Rosa Parks, the African American woman who became famous in 1955 for refusing to give up her bus seat to a white man. President John F. Kennedy appointed Daisy to the Democratic National Committee as well, where she worked for antipoverty programs, and to register black voters. Daisy threw herself into this job with the same dedication and persistence she applied to integrating Little Rock. In one city in Ohio, she got up on a bar stool and rallied the crowd to the point where they followed her out of the bar and down to the courthouse to register.

The year 1963 was one of the most eventful of the Civil Rights movement. Lunch counter sit-ins, freedom bus rides, where African Americans and their white supporters boarded segregated interstate buses, and equality marches and rallies were occurring throughout the United States. Daisy played a unique role in perhaps the most famous of these rallies, the historic march for civil rights, in Washington, D.C., where Martin Luther King, Jr. gave his famous "I Have a Dream" speech. Despite all her encounters with people who hated her, it was the anticipation of the short speech Daisy was asked to make here that was one of her most terrifying experiences. She had already met Martin Luther King at a fundraiser in New York, and she was honored to be invited to speak at the rally with this brilliant man. What scared her was that there were thousands of people and she had to speak right after the famous and highly esteemed Dr. King. Daisy was one of the only black women of her time ever to be asked to speak at such a rally. "I was more scared than with mobs [in Little Rock]," she later said.[10]

That pivotal year in the struggle for civil rights also saw a heinous crime in Birmingham, Alabama. A bomb was flung by whites into an African American church, killing four small girls who were there attending Sunday school and blinding another. Daisy befriended the blinded girl and took her under her wing. After a lengthy surgery partially corrected the vision in one eye, Daisy found a school for the visually impaired for the girl to attend.

Later that year, President John F. Kennedy was assassinated. America was shattered, and civil rights workers lost a great supporter. In a speech made a few days after his death, Daisy said, "President Kennedy, I believe, was trying always to teach us two fundamental lessons that must go with us now and for as long as the American nation and its people survive. The first lesson is that we are a great people with a great mission, and therefore in all things we must act like a great people. The second is that we truly are a nation, city and country, strong and weak, black and white, all together on the long journey. Thus, a sickness of spirit among one group will infect us all. Injustice practiced by or against some will poison us all. Weakness in one area will spread to others."[11]

When a new kind of adversity entered Daisy's life in 1965, it stopped her in her tracks. At the age of only fifty-one she suffered a major stroke which put her in the hospital for several weeks. Her speech and her hearing were permanently damaged. But Daisy Bates knew how to handle adversity better than most. Within two years, she was up and running again, to perform some of her most impressive work yet, in a place called Mitchellville.

Chapter 10

Mitchellville

Death threats didn't stop Daisy Bates, and life-threatening health obstacles couldn't slow her down for long. Daisy worked hard to overcome her stroke. She even managed to maintain her connections with the NAACP throughout her convalescence. By 1967, she was ready to tackle another project. She started working for the Arkansas Training Program of the Office of Economic Opportunity (OEO). This was a federal government agency that helped to eliminate poverty in the United States. One of the first places to catch Daisy's attention in her new position was called Mitchellville. It was an almost all-black, very small town of about 550 people in southern Arkansas, close to Huttig where Daisy had grown up.

The entire town of Mitchellville was about the size of thirty-seven football fields. In 1944, a Baptist church group had bought the land and sold it in pieces to poor black farm workers who had lost their jobs to new machines that could do farm work faster and for less money. Most of Mitchellville's residents weren't educated beyond their skills as farmers. They couldn't even read. For $50, they each bought a piece of the church land that was about as large as a school gymnasium.

It had been reported to the OEO that Mitchellville was really in dire straits. Daisy looked for a way to get a good survey of the town and its needs. She called a friend of hers, Dr. Bob Riley, who she thought could help. Dr. Riley taught political science at a Baptist university in Arkansas called Ouachita University. Political scientists study how governments manage the needs and problems of their people. Dr. Riley thought his students would be interested in this hands-on chance to learn about and experience political science in the field. He was right. Twenty-one of his students volunteered to make a hundred-mile trip to Mitchellville one rainy Saturday afternoon to talk to the residents.

What the students found during their survey was appalling. About one third of the families earned less than $1,000 a year and almost 100 percent earned less than $3,000. The income for an average family in the United States at that time was considerably greater than that of the average family in Mitchellville.

The poverty in Mitchellville was apparent at almost every level. None of the homes had flush toilets. Most of the homes used wood-burning stoves for cooking and for heat. None had vacuum cleaners, washing machines, or any of the other appliances that most people took for granted in the 60s. About the only convenience most of the families had was a television set. There was no place in the whole town for people to socialize, except for one small, crumbling room that was called a meeting hall, and one simple, all-purpose store. There was no community center, no police or fire department, no post office. There were no theaters, libraries, schools, doctor's offices, shopping malls, or restaurants.

Even with this knowledge beforehand, Daisy was disturbed by her first visit to Mitchellville. Many of the families she met were large; it wasn't unusual for a family of seven to sleep in two tiny rooms of a dilapidated shack that was nearly falling down. Townspeople would joke with newcomers that when it rained, they would go outside to keep dry. There were so many leaks in their roofs they were more likely to find a dry spot under a tree or an overhang outdoors. After walking through the town, Daisy said, "Something is drastically wrong with the [American] system when...our country with all her wealth can administer aid to foreign people and let her own [people] suffer."[1]

After the university students had interviewed the residents, they had a large town meeting with Dr. Riley, Daisy, and some of the people of Mitchellville, including the mayor. At the meeting Daisy offered to try to get outside funding for some critically needed improvements, like a sewerage system, some paved streets and repairs, and simple safety measures for the homes. One of the first priorities was to get running water to the homes, which would enable people to have flush toilets.

Daisy, Dr. Riley, and the Ouachita students decided that the best way to help the citizens of Mitchellville was to teach them to help themselves. Daisy felt that motivating people was the way to make sure they would succeed. "I don't care what anybody says, when you've motivated a community to help itself, you've performed a miracle," she said. "Without motivation, it doesn't matter what you give people."[2] She moved into a trailer in Mitchellville that doubled as her OEO office. Daisy lived and worked there during the week, and went home to L.C. on the weekends. The program that she and Dr. Riley started was called the Mitchellville OEO Self-Help Project.

Not too long after this, a six-year-old girl named Linda Mitchell befriended Daisy. All the children in Mitchellville loved Daisy, but Linda followed her everywhere. Linda's parents were separated, there were eight children in the family, and Linda's mother was thrilled to have her daughter spending so much time with such a learned and inspiring woman as Daisy Bates. Every day after school Linda went directly to Daisy's trailer to do her homework. Sometimes they would sit at the table together to work, and sometimes Daisy would just go about her personal business, fixing her hair, putting on makeup, or making dinner. Whatever she was doing, Daisy would teach Linda at the same time. She explained everything she did to Linda: how to set a table properly; how to use good table manners; how to act respectfully to adults. Even when Linda wanted to take a break and watch TV, Daisy made sure she only watched *Sesame Street*, because she could learn from that and have fun at the same time.

Linda was in the first grade when she met Daisy, and though she was very bright, when it was time for Linda to move to second grade the teacher didn't feel she was ready. Daisy wouldn't hear of it. She had just begun to work with Linda, and was certain that the child was second grade material. Daisy intensified her involvement in Linda's studies, quizzing her on all the letters as she taught Linda to read. Linda studied hard to make sure she knew the right answers, because Daisy was very serious about learning. Daisy took her complaint all the way up to the superintendent, and Linda was passed to second grade, where she proudly received straight A's. Later, when Linda was learning her times tables, Daisy would quiz her. Even if Linda got all the way up to the sixes and made one mistake, Daisy would say, "Okay, start all over again," and Linda would have to start again with the ones.

Linda didn't live with Daisy right away, but she spent so much time there that Daisy made a bedroom just for her. By the time Linda was in second grade, Daisy had asked her mom if she could just stay there all the time, and Linda's mom agreed. Linda's own house was small and crowded, and her mother was overwhelmed with the recent separation from her husband. Linda called Daisy "Mama Bates." Linda asked Daisy why she didn't have her own children, and Daisy told her she was unable to have children of her own but she sure loved them.

Daisy was strict, but she and Linda adored each other. Each morning Daisy would stride into Linda's small bedroom, and while she pulled the drapes back to let the sunlight in, she sang "Do-re-mi-

fa-so-la-ti..." and then she screamed, "DO!"³ Linda loved having sup-
per together, holding hands and saying grace before each meal. She
loved snuggling with Daisy's cat, Fluffy, who slept at the end of her
bed each night. She loved decorating the Christmas tree each winter
with Daisy. Together they would make popcorn strings, and then put
ribbons, red bows and the popcorn strings all around the tree, with a
star at the top. And every weekend they traveled back to Little Rock
to be with L.C.

Meanwhile, Dr. Riley and the Ouachita University students were
busy creating adult education classes, a reading clinic, a recreational
program for youth, and a leadership clinic for those people in
Mitchellville who were interested in learning how to govern the
town. Some of the adult education classes were based on sewing skills
the town women already had. Women who knew how to sew taught
others in the community how to mend old clothes, how to remake
adult clothes to fit children, and how to upholster old furniture to
make it look nice.

While the university students were busy creating the programs,
Daisy set to work finding the big money to fix the big problems. She
went from local to state agencies throughout Arkansas, presenting
the situation in Mitchellville, and the plans for improving it. While
her program was approved by both the state and regional agencies,
none of them funded it. Daisy was still not very popular in Arkansas.

Of course, that didn't stop Daisy. Next she went to Washington
and talked to people in charge of the United States government. Here
she found sympathy *and* federal money to change things. Right
before Daisy got involved with Mitchellville, water lines had been
installed there with the aid of a federal loan. Now the federal government said they would pay for sewerage lines to be put in, so that the
waste from the flush toilets they would install could be properly dis-
posed of. One thing led to another and within two years Mitchellville
citizens were staffing a new preschool program, building new homes,

and transforming the little town hall from an empty shack to a real office. They painted the walls, installed proper lights, and filled the space with purpose by adding tables, bookshelves, and desks.

Linda often traveled with Daisy and attended Daisy's important meetings during these years. Once, when they went to Texas, Daisy took her on an elevator for the first time and showed her how to use it. Daisy then asked her if she could do it on her own. Linda was thrilled to go by herself and push all those buttons. The problem was, she never paid much attention to where they got off the elevator and so she got lost on the way. When Daisy retrieved the sobbing child from the front desk, she didn't yell at her, but she said very sternly, "Don't *ever* say you know how to do something when you really don't."[4]

In a short time, Daisy's efforts began to pay off. With grant money she had coaxed from local and federal agencies, the Mitchellville residents planned a town community center. McGraw-Hill Publishing Company and the NAACP had already donated 5,000 books for the reading room. The community center was finished in 1972, and boasted a large swimming pool in addition to a daycare center, recreation area, kitchen facilities, and classrooms. After a few more years, the center acquired a pool table, a jukebox, and an assortment of games.

Another improvement Daisy helped implement was the creation of a health clinic in the community center. She called friends who were doctors, dentists, and midwives and persuaded them to donate their services in Mitchellville. Then she appealed to more hospitals and government agencies to get the proper equipment for the clinic.

Other money that had been provided for Mitchellville by Washington agencies was used to pay residents to fix up the town. Older people performed simple jobs like removing health hazards from the homes, while the younger men did construction work, painted, tiled floors and walls, and installed bathrooms in the homes, sewerage lines under the roads, and concrete pavement. Not only did this experience help renovate their town, and give them a source of pride, but it taught them skills that enabled them to remain independently employed.

Daisy wanted Mitchellville to have its own fire department, so she called and wrote letters to hundreds of people, searching for fire equipment. One day, she received notice that a fire truck was coming from New York. She was quite excited when the beautiful truck arrived, but it was so large, and would require so much money to fix and run, that they couldn't afford to use it. Finally, the fire chief in the Little Rock Fire Department was moved by Daisy's relentless efforts and worked out a way to help. Little Rock–the same city that had hissed after Daisy as she walked down the street only ten years before–was now sending Mitchellville its own fire truck, fully equipped with everything it needed, including fire resistant clothing and helmets, on Daisy's behalf! Little Rock also trained some Mitchellville residents as a squad of certified firemen.

Many of the early residents of Mitchellville were now elderly people who were suffering from health problems and could no longer fully take care of themselves. Daisy arranged for volunteers from church groups and other organizations, as well as other Mitchellville residents, to help the elderly. They started a Meals-on-Wheels program where a warm, nutritious noon meal was made and delivered to people who needed it, five days a week.

After a few years of living among the Mitchellville citizens, Daisy made an interesting discovery. Many of the older residents kept their life savings under their mattresses because they didn't know where else to put their hard-earned money. They didn't realize that in a bank the money would not only be safer but could earn them additional money. Daisy helped the town create a credit union that would assist residents in getting fair loans and learning how to wisely save and borrow money.

By 1974, after having Linda live with her for almost five years, Daisy loved the child as her own and asked Linda's mother if she could adopt her. But Linda's mother wanted her child back, and sent her brother to bring Linda back home. Daisy moved back to Little Rock that December. Only six years after her first visit, she had been responsible for acquiring more than two million dollars of donations for improvements in Mitchellville. The town was thriving and the citizens would never forget her.

"I don't know what this town would be like if not for Mrs. Bates. The town has changed almost completely," said one of the town leaders when Daisy left. "She instilled in us leadership ability so we could carry on."[5] Daisy's foster daughter, Linda, remained in contact with her for the rest of her life. "She taught me everything I know,"[6] Linda recalled in admiration.

Chapter 11

Freedom Sparks

In 1974, Daisy Bates left Mitchellville and officially retired. She was sixty years old. At the same time, a high school student in nearby Eldorado, Arkansas was dating a boy named Cleodis Gatson. The student, named Sharon Thigpen, had a girlfriend who was doing a school report on Daisy Bates. Sharon and her friend thought of Daisy as a living legend, and were excited to discover that Daisy was born and raised not far from where they lived. They wondered if she could be related to Sharon's boyfriend Cleodis, since they had the same last name.

Sharon asked Cleodis, and Cleodis asked his dad, who said that, yes, Daisy was his half-sister and Cleodis's aunt. He explained that Daisy's birth dad, Hezekiah C. Gatson, had moved north to Eldorado after Daisy's mother had died, and that he, Cleo Sr., was one of nine more children Daisy's father had had while living there.

Ten years later, in 1984, Sharon and Cleodis, now married with a six-year-old daughter, moved to Little Rock. They were sitting on the living room floor of their new home, thumbing through the phone book that had been delivered. They couldn't believe how thick it was compared to their tiny phone book from the little town of Eldorado. There were so many people in Little Rock!

Sharon had never forgotten about Daisy Bates. She took out the phone book and searched under "B." There she was, "Bates, Daisy," right in the Little Rock phone book with everybody else.

The first question Daisy asked Cleodis when he called, was, "How do you spell your last name?" Throughout Daisy's life, the few people who knew her birth father's name nearly always mispronounced and misspelled it as "Gaston." When Cleodis spelled the name correctly, Daisy said she'd love to meet him. He, Sharon, and their daughter Mia soon became a major part of Daisy's life.[1]

The year that Cleodis and Sharon came into Daisy's life was a very busy one, despite the fact that she was officially retired. Her husband, L.C., had died in 1980 and Daisy was determined to revive the *State Press* in his honor. "Even though I was very active in all kinds of activities to build up and strengthen the black communities in Arkansas, I never gave up hope that one day the *State Press* could reopen,"[2] she said.

Daisy revived the paper in 1984 and it became successful once again. With the help of the new editor, Ari Merretazon, the esteemed weekly paper reached a circulation of 11,000 copies in its first ten weeks of publication.

While Daisy was building up the *State Press* again, another exciting thing happened. Her autobiography, *The Long Shadow of Little Rock,* came back into print. Daisy had first written her life story in 1962. At that time the book wasn't very successful. Many of the people who read it said that Daisy sounded too bitter and angry. Her anger made them uncomfortable. As a result, the book didn't sell very well and went out of print. Twenty-four years later, the University of Arkansas thought that America was ready to hear Daisy's story and they reprinted it. They were right. *The Long Shadow of Little Rock* appeared back on book shelves in 1986, and finally received the recognition it deserved. In 1988, Daisy's book received the prestigious American Book Award from the Before Columbus Foundation. This award had been established ten years earlier to acknowledge the excellent cultural diversity of American writing and it was the first time ever that a reprinted book received that honor.

Because of the attention her book was getting, Daisy was united with many family members she had never even met. She also began receiving recognition for her lifetime of work in civil rights. In 1989, her achievements were honored in a national exhibit called, "I Dream a World: Portraits of Black Women Who Changed America," along with other famous African Americans like Rosa Parks, Marian Anderson, Lena Horne, and Oprah Winfrey. A cousin, Lenda Gatson Hunter, introduced Daisy to the vast new family her father had started when he moved to Eldorado. Daisy was delighted with all her relatives and the things she had in common with them. She had a lifetime of stories to catch up on. She had also amassed a lifetime of achievements that were still being recognized. She was honored as a torch carrier for the 1996 Olympics, and was frequently called on to give speeches in Little Rock schools and to give interviews for magazines and newspapers.

Daisy's achievements still shine in every place she touched. One need only drink in the colorful array of flowers blooming today in front of nearly every home in the little town of Mitchellville to be reminded of Daisy Bates's presence there. The OEO self-help project that Daisy began in 1968 is no longer active, but Mitchellville still receives grants every year from the United States Department of Housing and Urban Development (HUD). The town now boasts two of its own grocery stores, three churches, and two more daycare centers. Mitchellville even has its own police department. All of Mitchellville's young children attend school in nearby Dumas.

Today, Central High School in Little Rock is about 60 percent African American and 40 percent white. Many of the teachers are African American as well. Now, classes at Central High School include African American history and culture in the basic curriculum. Students often select Martin Luther King, Jr. as their chosen hero,

Keeping up her fight for civil rights, Daisy (left) boycotts a Woolworth store in New York City, 1962. *Photo by Gordon Anderson. Courtesy of the Wisconsin Historical Society, Daisy Bates Collection, Image # Whi-5004.*

Above: Daisy Bates and other guests are greeted at the White House by President John F. Kennedy, who appointed her to the Democratic National Committee. *Courtesy of Cecil Stoughton. Daisy Bates Papers (MC 582), Series 4, Subseries 4, Box 9, #57. Special Collections, University of Arkansas Libraries, Fayetteville.*

Left: Daisy loved children. Here she is with Linda Mitchell and an unidentified boy. *Daisy Bates Papers (MC 582), Series 4, Subseries 14, Box 11, #421. Special Collections, University of Arkansas Libraries, Fayetteville.*

Wheelchair-bound in her later years, Daisy was now a national treasure. She is holding the honorary torch from the 1996 Olympics. *Courtesy of Lenda Gatson Hunter.*

right along with Jesus Christ, Johann Sebastian Bach, Susan B. Anthony, William Shakespeare, and Daisy Gatson Bates. The well-respected presidents of the student body are often black. Central High holds a reputation as one of the best high schools in the nation.

Former president Bill Clinton was an eleven-year-old Arkansas resident in 1957 when Daisy Bates and the Little Rock Nine fought for their right to equal education. Forty years later, in 1997, he returned to Little Rock as President of the United States to honor Daisy Bates and the Little Rock Nine:

> When those nine black children were escorted by armed troops on their first day of school, there were a lot of people who were afraid to stand up for them. But the local NAACP, led by my friend Daisy Bates, stood up for them. Today, every time we take a stand that advances the cause of equal opportunity and excellence in education, every time we do something that really [helps eliminate poverty,] every time we further the cause of [promoting positive relationships among all the races,] we are honoring the spirit of Daisy Bates.[3]

To be sure, neither Central High, nor Little Rock, nor America is entirely free yet from discrimination and segregation. In a later speech about the integration of Little Rock schools, President Clinton said, "Today children of every race walk through the same door, but then they often walk down different halls. Not only in this school but across America, they sit in different classrooms, they eat at different tables. They even sit in different parts of the bleachers at the football game. Far too many communities are all white, all black, all Latino, all Asian. Indeed, too many Americans of all races have actually begun to give up on the idea of integration and the search for common ground.... Segregation is no longer the law, but too often, *separation* is still the rule.... There is still discrimination in America."[4]

Daisy was amazed by the impact that she and so many others made on civil rights, but she agreed with President Clinton that there was much room for improvement in race relations in the United States. In 1992, Daisy was interviewed for the Little Rock newspaper. The one goal she said she had not yet been able to achieve was full civil rights for all people. She was very concerned about "white flight" to the suburbs to avoid integrated schools. She wanted to see better housing and civil rights for poor blacks. And she felt that many of today's youth didn't understand or appreciate the strides their parents had made for civil rights. "What I'm afraid of is that what we did will be forgotten, that the children will never know what happened,"[5] she said.

Daisy Bates was proud of her achievements, and proud of the progress in civil rights that was achieved in her lifetime. In a speech she had made in the late 1960s she said, "If those of us who have felt the anguish of segregation and the pains of discrimination; and those of us who have tried to help a nation mold its morals, religion and politics—not by the sermons we preach but by the lives we live—would look around, we would see many freedom sparks glittering in the dark of despair like a flock of dancing lightning bugs whirling through the dark night of discrimination."[6]

Even during the most turbulent years of her life, Daisy believed that she could, and must, help Americans learn to live with one another, regardless of differences. She offered these words of wisdom to an audience of graduates about to go into the world as adults:

> Without love there is no life, but only an empty existence; and where love is limited and restricted—to one's own family circle or certain kinds of people only—then life is warped and spiritually crippled...Hatred is a two-edged sword; it harms the one who possesses it more than the one it is directed against...True civilization is a thing of the spirit.[7]

There was a time in 1957, at the height of the Little Rock crisis, when Daisy Bates could not drive up 14th Street to Central High School without fearing for her life. Today, that street is named in her honor. It is called Daisy L. Gatson Bates Drive. And the house that Daisy lived in with L.C. for thirty-two years, at 1207 West 28th Street in Little Rock, has been designated a National Historic Landmark.

Daisy Bates died on November 4, 1999, after a long struggle with her declining health. She was the first woman and African American in Arkansas history to lay in state at the Arkansas State Capitol, in an open coffin for mourners to come and pay their respects, without the prerequisite of being a state official. Among the visitors was Ernest Green, one of the Little Rock Nine, who has created his own highly esteemed place in the fabric of American society. "She was an enormous trailblazer," he said of Daisy. "She was someone ahead of her time. I think this community will really feel, as time goes on, the tremendous positive impact that Daisy and L.C. Bates will have had on the state of Arkansas."[8]

In 1996, Daisy Bates had visited the University of Arkansas during Black History Month. In closing the ceremony that honored her, the chancellor of the university, Mr. Dan Ferritor, asked, "Do heroes rise or does the time create them?... It was not the time that created Daisy Bates. It was Daisy Bates that created the time. She is a hero . . . We will not quit celebrating the legacy of Daisy Bates."[9]

Afterword

What Happened to the Little Rock Nine?

The Little Rock Nine changed America, and they were changed by the role they played in the Civil Rights movement. Here is what happened to each of them.

Ernest Green

Ernest was the only senior of the Little Rock Nine. He was the first African American to graduate from Central High School in Little Rock, on May 27, 1958. He attended Michigan State University, then served as the Assistant Secretary of Labor to President Jimmy Carter. He is now a managing partner and vice president of Lehman Brothers, an investment banking firm in Washington, D.C.

Elizabeth Eckford

Elizabeth was targeted from the start by segregationists, due to her exposure on that first, harrowing day she went to Central High School. Her mother was fired from her teaching job at the State School for the Blind in 1958, due to the integration issue. Elizabeth completed her high school studies through correspondence classes when Governor Faubus closed all the high schools in Little Rock. She attended college in Galesburg, Illinois and in Wilberforce, Ohio, then

joined the army. The only one of the Little Rock Nine to remain in
Little Rock, Elizabeth now lives with her two children and is a part-
time social worker.

Jefferson Thomas

Having given up his track star status and his position as president of the
student council before transferring to Central High School, Jefferson's
worst ordeal during that first year of integration was being struck so
hard on the head that he was rendered unconscious. He had a lump
the size of an egg when he awoke, but insisted on attending school
the next day to prevent further escalation by his attackers. One of
only three of the Little Rock Nine to graduate from Central High
School, Jefferson went on to college first at Wayne State University in
Detroit, Michigan, and then to City College in Los Angeles, California.
He is an accountant with the U.S. Department of Defense.

Dr. Terrence Roberts

Terrence and his family moved to Los Angeles, California at the end
of the 1957–58 school year, where he finished high school. He earned
his doctorate degree and became the Assistant Dean in the School of
Social Welfare at the University of California in Los Angeles, where
he currently teaches. He is also a clinical psychologist.

Carlotta Walls Lanier

Carlotta graduated from Central High School on May 30, 1960.
Carlotta's father, a brick mason, had to seek work out of state during
the Little Rock crisis because the building contractors in Little Rock
refused to hire him. Carlotta graduated from Michigan State
University in East Lansing, Michigan, and is now a real estate broker
in Denver, Colorado.

Minnijean Brown Trickey

Minnijean, after over four months of continuous harassment in 1957, finally retaliated for the second time, and was expelled from Central High School for doing so. The student body circulated cards that they all proudly wore saying, "one down, eight to go," as soon as she left. Daisy helped place Minnijean in New Lincoln High School, in New York City, where she was granted a scholarship. After graduating from New Lincoln, Minnijean attended Mt. Sinai School of Nursing, then transferred to Southern Illinois University. She is a writer and is involved in environmental causes.

Gloria Ray Karlmark

Gloria's attackers during the 1957–58 school year chose to torment her psychologically, for the most part. In anonymous calls they threatened to lynch her, to squirt acid in her face, and in the halls they lit firecrackers behind her that sounded like gunfire. Gloria's mother was forced to resign her job that year because her daughter was one of "the nine." Gloria went on to graduate from the Illinois Institute of Technology in Chicago, Illinois, and received her post-doctorate degree in Stockholm, Sweden. She was a computer science writer, and now splits her time between homes in the Netherlands and Stockholm, where her husband's family lives.

Thelma Mothershed Wair

Thelma experienced less harassment than the other students, due to the well-known fact at the time that she suffered from a serious heart condition. This reprieve still was not sufficient to prevent several minor heart attacks during the integration crisis, however. Thelma completed her high school studies through correspondence classes when the high schools in Little Rock were shut down, then attended Southern Illinois University in Carbondale, Illinois. She settled down and became a school counselor in East St. Louis, Illinois. Currently, she lives in Belleville, Illinois, where she is a volunteer in a program for abused women.

Melba Pattillo Beals

Melba attended San Francisco State University in California and became the head of a public relations firm there. She is an author and former journalist for *People* magazine and NBC, and still lives in San Francisco.

The schools in Little Rock were not fully integrated until 1973. In 1987, thirty years after the first attempt to integrate Central High School, the Little Rock Nine returned for a reunion celebration. They were given a hero's welcome—a far cry from the harassment of 1957. In November, 1999, coincidentally on the day Daisy Bates was buried, the Little Rock Nine were awarded the Congressional Medal of Honor, the highest award that can be bestowed on a civilian, by President Clinton in Washington, D.C.

Notes

1. Opportunity Knocks

1. Daisy Bates. *The Long Shadow of Little Rock* (Fayetteville: University of Arkansas Press, 1962) p. 70; Melba Pattillo Beals. *Warriors Don't Cry* (New York: Pocket Books, 1994) p. 37; Richard Kelso. *Days of Courage, The Little Rock Story* (Austin, Tex.: Raintree Steck-Vaughan, 1993) p. 20.

2. Kelso, *Days of Courage,* p. 18.

3. Lerone Bennett, Jr. "Chronicles of Black Courage: The Little Rock 10," *Ebony,* vol. 53, no. 2 (Dec. 1997): p. 135.

2. Huttig

1. Peter Irons. *The Courage of Their Convictions* (New York, The Free Press, 1988) p. 117.

2. Bates, *Long Shadow,* p. 13.

3. Ibid., p. 8.

4. Irons, *Courage,* p. 117–18.

5. Bates, *Long Shadow,* p. 8.

3. Shattered Innocence

1. Bates, *Long Shadow,* p. 10.

2. Ibid., p. 14.

3. Ibid.

4. Ibid., p. 18.

5. Ibid., p. 19.

4. Revenge

1. Bates, *Long Shadow,* p. 17.
2. Ibid., p. 19–20.
3. Bennett, "Chronicles," p. 135.

5. Birth of the State Press

1. Irons, *Courage,* p. 120.
2. Daisy Bates, undated speech. Daisy Bates Collection, call #523 (Mss.), box 3, file 8, Wisconsin Historical Society, Madison, Wisc.
3. Bennett, "Chronicles," p. 138.
4. Sanford Wexler. *The Civil Rights Movement, An Eyewitness History* (New York: Facts on File, 1993) p. 9.
5. Bates, *Long Shadow,* p. 36.
6. Ibid., p. 41.

6. Days of Change

1. Linda S. Caillouet. "Daisy Lee Gatson Bates," *Arkansas Democrat-Gazette,* Jan. 12, 1992, p. 6.
2. Darren Rhym. *The NAACP* (Philadelphia, Pa.: Chelsea House Publishers, 2002) p. 68.
3. This is not an actual quote, but a summary of the anti-integration senti-ment expressed in hundreds of letters in the Daisy Bates Collection at the Wisconsin Historical Society, box 1, file 2; and in James Tackach. *Brown vs. Board of Education* (San Diego: Calif.: Lucent Books, 1998) p. 93; as well as several of the other sources cited in these notes.
4. Bates, *Long Shadow,* p. 48.

7. Tension Builds in Little Rock

1. Laurie A. O'Neill. *Little Rock: The Desegregation of Central High* (Brookfield, Conn.: Millbrook Press, 1994) p. 23.
2. Bates, *Long Shadow,* p. 4.
3. Ibid., p. 57.
4. Irons, *Courage,* p. 111.
5. Wexler, *Civil Rights Movement,* p. 97.

8. Chaos in Little Rock

1. Beals, *Warriors,* p. 35.
2. O'Neill, *Little Rock,* p. 25.
3. Beals, *Warriors,* p. 46.
4. Kelso, *Days of Courage,* p. 35.

5. Beals, *Warriors,* p. 72.

6. "Daisy Bates: There's Still a CR 'Need'," *Sentinel-Record,* June 6, 1976, p. 40.

7. Bates, *Long Shadow,* p. 96.

8. O'Neill, *Little Rock,* p. 37.

9, Daisy Bates Collection, call #523, Wisconsin Historical Society, box 1, file 2.

10. Bates, *Long Shadow,* p. 171.

9. Ripples from Little Rock

1. Daisy Bates, undated speech. Daisy Bates Collection, call #523, Wisconsin Historical Society, box 3, file 8.

2. "History of Little Rock Public Schools Desegregation," http://www.cen-tralhigh57.org/1957–58. htm, 1997.

3. Scott Flanagin. "Celebrating a Legacy," *NW Arkansas Times*, Feb. 28, 1996, p. A6.

4. "The Arkansas Terror Campaign Against Daisy Bates," *Jet Magazine*, Oct. 23, 1958, p. 17.

5. Ibid., p. 16.

6. Daisy Bates Papers. (MC 582) series 1, subseries 3, box 3, file 7; Honors and Awards, Nov. 1957–July 1981; Special Collections, University of Arkansas Libraries, Fayetteville.

7. Bates, *Long Shadow,* p. 168.

8. Ibid., p. 178.

9. Ibid., p. 212.

10. Caillouet, "Daisy Lee Gatson Bates," p. 6.

11. Daisy Bates, undated speech. Daisy Bates Collection, call #523, Wisconsin Historical Society, series 3, subseries 2, box 3, file 6.

10. Mitchellville

1. "Mitchellville OEO Self-Help Project," Daisy Bates Papers, series 3, subseries 2, box 6, file 5, Special Collections, University of Arkansas Libraries, Fayetteville.

2. Marion Humphrey. "Mrs. Bates Worries About the Future of Mitchellville Self-Help Program," *Pine Bluff Commercial,* April 15, 1973.

3. Interview with Linda Mitchell, Jan. 17, 1999.

4. Ibid.

5. James Merriweather. "Mitchellville Is Growing Monument to One Woman's Vision, Leadership," *Arkansas Gazette*, May 4, 1975.

6. Linda Mitchell, Jan. 17, 1999.

11. Freedom Sparks

1. Discussions with Sharon Gatson, wife of Daisy's half-nephew, Cleodis Gatson, and Daisy's cousin Lenda Gatson Hunter, on Nov. 8, 1999 and Aug. 29, 2002.

2. Irons, *Courage,* p. 127.

3. "Transcript of Remarks by President Clinton to NAACP National Convention," July 17, 1997, http://usinfo.state.gov/usa/blackhis/naacp.htm

4. "The White House: Remarks by the President in Ceremony Commemorating the 40th Anniversary of the Desegregation of Central High School," Little Rock, Ark., September 25, 1997. http://usinfo.state-gov/usa/blackhis/1997092a.htm

5. "Daisy Bates: There's Still a CR Need," p. 40.

6. Daisy Bates, undated speech. Daisy Bates Collection, Wisconsin Historical Society, box 3, file 6.

7. Ibid., box 3, file 8.

8. "Mourners Pay Tribute to Daisy Bates," *Arkansas Democrat-Gazette*, Nov. 9, 1999, p. 8A.

9. Cecille Doan. "The Ultimate in Role Models," *Razorback*, 1996, p. 54.

Selected Bibliography

Archives

Daisy Bates Collection (MSS) 532, donated 1966, University of Wisconsin Historical Society, Madison, Wisconsin

Daisy Bates Papers. (MC 582), donated 1986. Special Collections, University of Arkansas Libraries, Fayetteville, Arkansas

Daisy Bates, Daisy Bates Papers, Correspondence, Memorabilia, Photographs, Newspaper Clippings, Audio Tapes and Film, 1948–1986, Manuscript Collection MC 582, http://cavern.uark.edu/libinfo/ speccoll/batesaid.html

Books

Bates, Daisy. *The Long Shadow of Little Rock*. Fayetteville: University of Arkansas Press, 1986

Beals, Melba Pattillo. *Warriors Don't Cry*. New York: Pocket Books, 1994

Haskins, Jim. *I Have a Dream–the Life and Words of Martin Luther King, Jr.* Brookfield: Conn.: Millbrook Press, 1992

Haskins, Jim. *Separate But Not Equal: The Dream and the Struggle*. New York: Scholastic Press, 1998

Irons, Peter. *The Courage of Their Convictions*. New York: The Free Press, 1988

Lusane, Clarence. *The Struggle for Equal Education, African-American Experience*. Danbury, Conn.: Franklin Watts, 1992

McKissack, Patricia and Frederick. *The Civil Rights Movement in America from 1865 to the Present*. Chicago: Children's Press, 1987

O'Neill, Laurie A. *Little Rock: The Desegregation of Central High*. Brookfield, Conn.: Millbrook Press, 1994

Rhym, Darren. *The NAACP.* Philadelphia, Pa.: Chelsea House, 2002

Rochelle, Belinda. *Young People Who Fought for Civil Rights.* New York: Lodestar Books, 1993

Severance, John B. *Gandhi, Great Soul.* New York: Clarion Books, 1997

Takach, James. *Brown vs. Board of Education.* San Diego, Calif.: Lucent Books, 1998

Wexler, Sanford. *The Civil Rights Movement, An Eyewitness History.* New York: Facts on File, 1993

Magazines and Newspapers

"The Arkansas Terror Campaign Against Daisy Bates," *Jet Magazine,* Oct. 23, 1958, pp. 14–17

Bayani, Elsa, and Kearney, Janis. "Daisy L. Bates Celebrates 80th Birthday," J. D. Hyman, Inc., Little Rock, Ark., Nov. 12, 1994, Program for birthday celebration

Bennett, Lerone, Jr. "Chronicles of Black Courage: The Little Rock 10," *Ebony,* Dec. 1997, vol. 53, no. 2, p. 132(5)

Bennett, Lerone, Jr. "First Lady of Little Rock," *Ebony,* Sept. 1958, pp. 17–24

Caillouet, Linda S. "Daisy Lee Gatson Bates," *Arkansas Democrat-Gazette,* Jan. 12, 1992, p. 6

"Daisy Bates: There's Still a CR 'Need'," *Sentinel-Record,* (Hot Springs National Park, Ark.) June 6, 1976, p. 40

Flanagin, Scott. "Celebrating a Legacy," *NW Arkansas Times,* Feb. 28, 1996, p. A1(A6)

Gosnell, Kathy. "Mitchellville: Desha County Negro Community with an Eye on the Future," *Pine Bluff Commercial,* March 16, 1969, p. 19/21

Humphrey, Marion. "Mrs. Bates Worries About the Future of Mitchellville Self-Help Program," *Pine Bluff Commercial,* April 15, 1973

"Light in a Dark Corner; A Story of the Origins of the Huttig Operations," *American Lumberman,* Jan. 28, 1905. Courtesy of Manville Forest Product Corporation, Huttig, Ark. 1987

Merriweather, James. "Mitchellville Is Growing Monument to One Woman's Vision, Leadership," *Arkansas Gazette,* May 4, 1975

"Mitchellville Makes Its Miracle," *The Action,* June 1972, vol. 3, no. 6, p. 1 (3,4)

"Mourners Pay Tribute to Daisy Bates," *Arkansas Democrat-Gazette,* Nov. 9, 1999, p. 1 (8A)

"New Role for Little Rock's Daisy Bates," *Jet Magazine,* April 2, 1964, pp. 14–21

"OEO Begins Project of 'Meals on Wheels'," *Dumas Clarion,* Nov. 24, 1971, section b, vol. 41, no. 53

Pappas, Brynda. "L.C. Bates: A Champion of Freedom," *Arkansas Gazette*, Oct. 19, 1980, p. 1E (4E)

Shores, Elizabeth F. "Civil Rights Activists Pay Respects to L.C. Bates at Services," *Arkansas Democrat*, Aug. 28, 1980, p. 13A

"The Story of Little Rock–As Governor Faubus Tells It," *U. S. News & World Report*, June 20, 1958, pp. 101–06

Stover, Bob. "Mrs. Daisy Bates Tackles Challenge–Mitchellville," *Arkansas Gazette*, Oct. 12, 1970, p. 3A

Stover, Bobby and James, Lamar. "Ouachita Students Will Aid Mitchellville," *Arkansas Gazette*, filed in Daisy Bates Papers, University of Arkansas Libraries, series 5, subseries 6, box 12, folder 14, Special Collections, Fayetteville, Ark.

Trescott, Jacqueline. Update, "'They can't make a murderer out of me,' she'd said. Now, 20 years later, Daisy Bates has a few kind words for the city of Little Rock," *Washington Post*, July 17, 1977

"Whatever Happened to Daisy Bates?" *Ebony*, vol. 39, Sept. 1984, p. 92 (94)

Interviews by Author

Sharon Gatson and Lenda Gatson Hunter, Little Rock, Ark., November 8, 1999 and August 29, 2002. Telephone interviews and letters.

Linda Mitchell, telephone interviews, January 17, 1999.

Internet

Daisy Bates, Daisy Bates Papers, Correspondence, Memorabilia, Photographs, Newspaper Clippings, Audio Tapes and Film, 1948–1986, Manuscript Collection MC 582, http://cavern.uark.edu/libinfo/speccoll/batesaid/batesaid.html

"History of Little Rock Public Schools Desegregation," http://www.centralhigh57.org/1957–58.htm, 1997

"Pioneer Women Honored for 'Shining' Achievements," *Atlanta Inquirer*, Nov. 9, 1996, http://www.usc.edu.au/library/database/ejournal/At-AusB.htm

"Transcript of Remarks by President Clinton to NAACP National Convention," July 17, 1997, http://usinfo.state.gov/usa/blackhis/naacp.htm

"The White House: Remarks by the President in Ceremony Commemorating the 40th Anniversary of the Desegregation of Central High School," Sept. 25, 1997, http://usinfo.state.gov/usa/blackhis/1997092a.htm

Further Reading

Kelso, Richard. *Days of Courage, The Little Rock Story*. Austin, Tex.: Raintree
  Steck-Vaughan, 1993

LeVine, Ellen. *Freedom's Children, Young Civil Rights Activists Tell Their Own
  Stories*. New York: G.P. Putnam's Sons, 1993

O'Neill, Laurie A. *Little Rock: The Desegregation of Central High*. Brookfield,
  Conn.: Millbrook Press, 1994

Parks, Rosa and Haskins, Jim. *Rosa Parks: My Story*. New York: Dial Books,
  1992

Rochelle, Belinda. *Young People Who Fought for Civil Rights*. New York: Lodestar
  Books, 1993

Index

Pages with illustrations are italicized.

African American, first use of terms in text: African American, 1; black, 1; Black American, 29; "Boy," 28; "Girl," 28; Negro, 7; nigger, 1; nigra, 28

African American(s): civil rights of, 28–29, 32, 34, 37, 55, 56, 66–67, 71, 73, 84, 88–89; crimes against, 13, 29, 32–33, 59, 66; "Nigra town," 8; threats to, 1–5, 6, 11, 15, 28, 29, 33, 39, 43–55, 58–59, 65, 66–73; in World War II, 29–32. *See also* Civil Rights movement; Discrimination; Race relations; Segregation

American Book Award, 83

Anderson, Marian, 84

Arkansas National Guard, 1, 46, 51, 54, 56, 62

Arkansas State Capitol, 90

Arkansas State government, 39–40, 64, 68

Arkansas State Police, 31, 46

Arkansas State Press, 30–34, 35, *50, 63, 70–71, 83*

Arkansas Training Program. *See* Office of Economic Opportunity

Auten, Lawrence C., 33

Bates, Daisy Lee Gatson: adoptive parents, 6–13, 18–22, 23; arrests, 34, 64, 70; autobiography, 72, 83; birth, 6; birth parents, 6, 12, 13–14, 17–18, 82, 84; childhood, 6–15; and children, 36, 63, 76–78, *86;* civil rights activities, 2–5, 30–34, 35–36, 38–70, 71–73, 74–81, *85;* death, 90; education, 8, 35; health, 73–74, 90; hobbies, 9, 14, 35; honors and awards, 69, 71, 84, *87;* and Little Rock Nine, 2–5, 38–72; marriage, 25, 70; and Mitchellville, 74–81; photos of, *frontis., 21, 47–49, 85–87;* quoted, 7, 10, 12, 14, 15, 26, 27, 36, 59, 67, 68, 71, 72, 73, 76, 79, 83, 89; threats to, 2, 41, 44–45, 46, 55, 59–63, 68, 70. *See also* Little Rock Nine

Bates, Lucius Christopher (L.C.) (husband), *21,* 46, *49,* 51, *52,* 55, 59, 63,

65, 68, 90; civil rights agenda, 23, 30–34, 70–71; death, 83; early years, 23–35; marriage, 25, 70; professional aspirations, 23–25, 30–34, 70–71; quoted, 23, 51

Beals Pattillo, Melba. *See* Pattillo, Melba

Before Columbus Foundation, 83–84

Birmingham, Ala., 73

Black. *See* African American

Blossom, Virgil, 38, 40, 41, 43, 51, 54, 55, 64

Boycotts, 44, 61, *85*; of *Arkansas State Press*, 32, 70

Brown v. the Topeka Board of Education, 36–39, 40, 66, 71

Brown, Minnijean, 42, *47, 50*, 93. *See also* Little Rock Nine

Buses: freedom, 72; integration of, 66; segregation on, 27, 29, 72

Carter, Jimmy, 91

Central High School, 1–5, 39–72, 84, 88, 91–94. *See also* Little Rock Nine

Cherry, Francis A., 38

Civil Rights movement, 34, 36–38, 56, 66–68, 71–73, *85*, 88–89, 91. *See also* Race relations

Civil War, 3, 41

Clinton, Bill, 88, 94

Clyde (foster child), 63

Cobb, Osro, 54–55

Commissary. *See* Union Saw Mill Company

Committee to Retain Our Segregated Schools (CROSS), 69

Congressional Medal of Honor, 94

Daisy L. Gatson Bates Drive (Little Rock), 90

Davies, Ronald N., 45, 51, 56–57

Democratic National Committee, 72, 86

Demonstrations, public, 1, *19*, 33, *49*, 53–54, 58, 62, 66–67, 71–73, *85*

Discrimination, 27, 28, 30, 31, 40, 88–89. *See also* Race relations; Segregation

"Drunken Pig," 17–22; death of, 18

Dumas, Ark., 84

Eckford, Elizabeth, 1–4, *19*, 42, *47, 50*, 52–53, 91–92. *See also* Little Rock Nine

Eisenhower, Dwight D., 59, 62, 70

Eldorado, Ark., 82, 84

Faubus, Orval, 38–39, 45, 46, *49*, 51, 56–57, 62, 68, 91

Federal Bureau of Investigation (FBI), 45, 55

Federal government, 28, 40–41, 59, 74, 78–79

Ferritor, Dan, 90

Foster, Thomas P., 32

Gandhi, Mahatma, 21, 44

Gatson, Daisy. *See* Bates, Daisy Lee Gatson

Gatson, Cleodis, 82–83

Gatson, Hezekiah (birth father), 6, 12, 13–14, 82, 84

Gatson, Mia, 83

Gatson, Sharon, 82–83

Glover, Albert, 32

Great Depression, 31

Green, Ernest, 42, *47, 50*, 67, 90, 91. *See also* Little Rock Nine

Guards. *See* Arkansas National Guard

Hay, A.J., 32
Horne, Lena, 34
Hunter, Lenda Gatson, 84
Huttig, Ark., 6, 7, 9, 13, 16, 22, 74

"I Dream a World: Portraits of Black
  Women," 84
Integration, 38–72, 88, 91–94; oppo-
  sition to, 3, 56, 61, 96; support for,
  56, 58, 60, 64, 90, 94. *See also*
  Little Rock Nine; Race relations;
  Segregation

Jim Crow laws, 40, 71

Karlmark, Gloria Ray. *See* Ray, Gloria
Kennedy, John F., 72, *86*; assassi-
  nated, 73
King, Martin Luther, Jr., 21, 44, 69,
  72, 84
Ku Klux Klan, 29, 41, 48, 55

Lanier, Carlotta Walls. *See* Walls,
  Carlotta
Lemley, Judge, 45, 67
Little Rock, Ark., 1–5, 31, 36, 38, 40,
  42–72, 80–81, 84, 88, 91–94
Little Rock Nine, 1–5, 42–72, 91–94;
  Daisy's role with, 2–5, 38–72;
  honors and awards, 69; parents
  of, 42, 69, 91–94; preparation for
  integration, 42–57; subsequent
  lives, 91–94; support for, 56,
  64–65; threats to, 1–4, 42–54, 55,
  56, 58–69. *See also* Brown,
  Minnijean; Eckford, Elizabeth;
  Green, Ernest; Mothershed,
  Thelma; Pattillo, Melba; Ray,
  Gloria; Roberts, Terrence;
  Thomas, Jefferson; Walls, Carlotta

Little Rock School Board, 38, 39,
  67
Long Shadow of Little Rock, The
  (Bates), 72, 83
Lynching, 1, 29, 54, 59, 71, 93

Mann, Woodrow Wilson, 46, 58, 59
March for civil rights (1963), 72
Marshall, Thurgood, 36–37, 64
Merretazon, Ari, 83
Miller, John, 39
Mitchell, Linda, 76–78, 79, 81
Mitchellville, Ark., 74–81, 84
Mothers League, 45
Mothershed, Thelma, 42, *47*, 93–94.
  See also Little Rock Nine

National Association for the
  Advancement of Colored People
  (NAACP), 36–37, 38, 39, 40, 63,
  71; Arkansas Conference, 36, 63;
  Daisy's role in, 30, 35–36, 38–40,
  45–51, 63–64, 67, 69, 74, 79; ori-
  gin and purpose, 28–30, 69; youth
  council, 36
National Guard. *See* Arkansas
  National Guard
National Historic Landmark, 90
Negro. *See* African American
Nigger. *See* African American
Nigra. *See* African American

Office of Economic Opportunity
  (OEO), 74; Self-Help Project, 76,
  84
Ogden, Dunbar, 52–54, 70
Olympics (1996), 84, 87
101st Airborne Infantry of United
  States Army, 4, 62, 64
Ouachita University, 75–76, 78

Parks, Rosa, 72, 84
Passive resistance, 44, 67; *See also*
    King, Martin Luther, Jr.; Gandhi,
    Mahatma
Pattillo, Melba, 42, *47, 50,* 53, 94. *See
    also* Little Rock Nine
Plessy v. Fergusson, 37

Race relations, 3, 7–9, 13, 14–16, 24,
    26, 28–29; racism in, 9, 24, 30, 33,
    44; separation in, 2, 5, 7–9, 25, 27,
    37, 56. *See also* Discrimination;
    Integration; Segregation
Racism. *See* Race relations
Ray, Gloria, 42, *47, 50,* 93. *See also*
    Little Rock Nine
Riley, Bob, 75–76, 78
Riley, Millie (birth mother), 6, 12;
    death of, 13–14
Roberts, Terrence, 42, *47, 50,* 92. *See
    also* Little Rock Nine
Robinson, Jackie, 25
Roosevelt, Eleanor, 72

Segregation, 2–3, 5, 7–8, 28, 31,
    36–40, 72. *See also* Race relations;
    Discrimination
Segregationists, 42–45, 55, 57–59, 62,
    63, 66, 69, 71, 88, 89, 91
Sit-ins, 66, 71, 72
Shotgun house, 8, *20*
Slavery, 3, 28
Smith, Orlee (adoptive father), 6, 7,
    12–15, 18, 22; quoted, 5, 23–24
Smith, Susie (adoptive mother), 7,
    10, 12–14, 18
Soldiers. *See* 101st Airborne Infantry
    of the United States Army; World
    War II

Spingarn Medal, 69
States rights v. federal rights, 40, 41
Strike, of cotton oil mill, 33
Supreme Court. *See* United States
    Supreme Court

Thigpen, Sharon. *See* Gatson,
    Sharon
Thomas, Jefferson, 42, *47, 50,* 92. *See
    also* Little Rock Nine
Threats. *See* African Americans;
    Bates, Daisy Lee Gatson; Little
    Rock Nine
Trickey, Minnijean Brown. *See*
    Brown, Minnijean

Union Saw Mill Company, 6–7, 8, 9,
    13, *20*; Commissary of, 7, 9, 15,
    17–22
United States Department of
    Housing and Urban Development
    (HUD), 84
United States government. *See*
    Federal government
United States Supreme Court, 36–38,
    40, 51, 64, 68–69
University of Arkansas, 83, 90

Voter registration, 72

Walls, Carlotta, 42, *47, 50,* 92. *See also*
    Little Rock Nine
Warren, Earl, 37
Washington, Val J., 64
Winfrey, Oprah, 84
Women's Emergency Committee to
    Save Our Schools (WEC), 69
World War II, 29, 20, 31–32; race
    and, 29–32